Walking
Alison

www.mascotbooks.com

Walking Alison: A Poodle's Mostly True Story of Helping Her Human Navigate Life

The author has tried to recreate events, locales, and conversations from their memories of them. In order to maintain their anonymity in some instances, the author has changed the names of individuals and places, and may have changed some identifying characteristics and details such as physical properties, occupations, and places of residence.

Author photo credit: Yolanda Perez

For more information, please contact:
Mascot Books, an imprint of Amplify Publishing Group
620 Herndon Parkway, Suite 220
Herndon, VA 20170
info@amplifypublishing.com

Library of Congress Control Number: 2023905192
CPSIA Code: PRV0623A
ISBN-13: 978-1-63755-820-1
Printed in the United States

For David and Grace, and my remarkable dog, Dea,
whose love of life makes my life so joyful.

Walking Alison

A Poodle's Mostly True Story
of Helping Her Human
Navigate Life

Alison Rand

MASCOT
BOOKS
an imprint of Amplify Publishing Group

Contents

The Beginning

Later, much later, after Alison had taken me into her home and her life, she told me that I was born on her birthday, April 2. All I know for sure is that my first memory was of lying next to my poodle mama and some scrabbling, groping, slimy, slightly furry creatures. I was the baby, the only female, and I came out with a surprising color—black! A lady picked me up and turned me over. Hey, what are you doing? You can't just pick me up like that and—

"This black girl has a gray marking on her chest and under her chin," said the lady, peering at me over her glasses. "The others are brown with no markings."

Is that a good thing, that I'm different already, before I have even opened my eyes? I have decided yes, it must be a good thing. I am already a special puppy; this much is clear.

One of the puppies wasn't wriggling around like the rest of us. They came and took him away. "Too small and delicate," the lady said. "Poor little guy. He's on his way to the Rainbow Bridge."

What's a rainbow? What's a bridge?

Wait, forget all that—what is that charming smell on the lady's fingers? It's pungent! Quite stimulating, actually. What can it be? I think it's a food item, but I can't seem to place it.... Well, I've only had a few things to smell so far, and I've got about three memories in the memory bank. I'm going to need more clues if they expect me to solve such deep mysteries of life.

I'm trying to get a sense of my surroundings. Let's see ... I am lying on newspaper, and I have to report right up front that this is not very comfortable. This is not what I expected. Well, I don't know what I expected, but this newspaper certainly isn't it. Didn't they just say I was special? That I was black, not brown like the others? Actually, now that I think this over, I'm feeling a bit confused because I really cannot see *anything*. No black, no brown. My eyes are still mostly shut. I feel my way with a little nudge from the lady with the odor on her fingers as I inch over to my poodle mama. She is lying on a comfier surface with padding inside a covered type of metal box. I try to get in prime position before my two brothers get there. They are busy licking each other and I block their way, hah! If they want to feed first, they will have to pay more attention. Do not underestimate me! No sirree! Oops, I just tumbled over ... and now I'm up again! Triumph!

There's so much to do around these parts—wrestle with my brothers, sleep, pee on the bad newspaper, sleep some more, and jockey for position when it's time to feed. After having my fill, I pee, curl up into the tiniest ball, and snooze. Busy, busy!

I don't know how much time has passed. A lot? A little? My eyes are fully open now. There's plenty going on out here! I look forward to seeing the lady and smelling her strong odor. She certainly is an odd one, because I can't tell what she's all about. She doesn't provide milk. She doesn't seem to pee or nap. She doesn't wrestle. What a lonely, hollow existence she must have. Instead, she brings over short, yappy humans, who are very loud and clumsy, and who try to poke their fingers at me.

"Be careful of the puppies, kids," the lady says. They like to look at my brothers and me and giggle. Every time we tumble over each other, they howl and laugh. When they come close enough to touch me, I kiss them on their noses, which makes them squeal. Is there something wrong with them? I have to admit, though, I enjoy the excited sound they make. Clearly, they think I am very special, because for everything I do, they make that noise. I have to admire their energy! I am going to make a little mental note of this, that tiny people are fun and they have a great attitude toward me. I can hone my innate comic abilities on them. They acknowledge, as I have suspected since the day I was born on Alison's birthday, that I am the center of the universe.

"Don't take them out of the crate," the woman tells the kids. Is this a crate? Will this be my new life? It feels pretty good so far. I can play with my squirmy brothers any time I like, and I feel safe and protected when I'm huddled with them in one big, squirmy ball.

The lady also visits the crate sometimes without the giggling little humans and strokes all of us, even my poodle mama. Sometimes she rubs behind my ears, and it feels really good! I reach up and kiss her on her nose. I am a good kisser.

But then, after giving me such a nice rub, comes the worst thing *ever* to happen in my entire life—the lady leaves! That's right, whenever she's done with her visit, she stops petting us and *she leaves the room*. I moan and cry until I cry myself to sleep. I can't help it! What have I done to merit such harsh treatment? Was I a bad puppy? But she kept saying I was a *good* puppy! Why does she have to leave *me*?! My brothers don't seem to notice, but I don't like it at all. Even after a nap, I remember that I've been utterly abandoned and I scrabble frantically around the newspaper, hoping the lady will come back soon. Surely if I cry again, she will hear my urgent plea.

If I were to think it through, perhaps I would remember that this happens all the time—the lady shows up, she scratches me behind the ear, she goes away, and eventually she comes back again. But that is a very long train of thought, and I am a very tiny puppy, and all I know is that the lady has abandoned me, no doubt for the rest of time.

Here's an idea, one of my very first—I can get my poodle mama to nestle me! I am the cutest: I am black with a gray marking on my chest and under my chin, and she will just have to nestle me.

But my poodle mama is resting. She is not interested in nuzzling me, and she can't scratch me behind the ear like the lady does.

My brief little life is over before it has truly begun.

A Special Puppy

There was one special dog before me. This is what I later heard.

Alison was always partial to poodles, ever since Remington—"Remmy"—and Natasha, the black poodles of her childhood.

"You know how things like that stay with you," Alison later told me, although I did not know what she was talking about because I was too new to have things stick that long.

"They don't shed," Alison would tell people when they asked why she was so partial to poodles, because poodles like me have hair, not fur. Also, we are super smart and bursting with pride and personality, and we're fun. . . . Well, all that goes without saying. So, when Alison talks about how we don't shed, she's hiding all the love and pain that comes with attachment. My opinion, sure, but I have good opinions—I've had several so far, and they are very science-based and full of poodle wisdom.

Who can say why one breed of dog touches someone's heart? When Alison's parents separated when she was six years old, they split up the kids the way breeders split up the litter—different ones to different homes, no rhyme or reason, just the way it eventually happened with my brothers and me. Alison's older sister and brother went off to live with their father in a new apartment in Manhattan. After three years of separation, Alison's

5

mother took her and Remmy the poodle to Las Vegas until the divorce was final. Remmy was Alison's only friend for a while. Maybe that's why she's got this poodle fixation, not that I disagree with her excellent taste.

Alba came along when Alison was fully grown. Dark chocolate, large for a miniature, unlike me. You can have poodles all your life, but then one special one comes along, and for Alison, that was Alba, my sister in heaven.

It turns out that Alison never went back to the neighborhood park for weeks after she lost Alba. Not only was Alison her poodle's number one mama and caretaker; she also became Alba's nurse day and night toward the end.

It seems Alba suffered from one thing after another during her fourteen years, two months, and six days of life, before she crossed over the Rainbow Bridge. I now know that is where all dogs go when they finally leave the park. They cross the bridge to a place where they can run free in lush meadows and the grassiest pastures filled with wildflowers. They chase dozens of *squirrels* that clamber up trees to rummage for their nuts. They hear the songs of chirping birds and they get to be with all the other dog friends who long ago left the park and never came back. If a human hears the term "Rainbow Bridge," their eyes water and they get the sniffly nose.

Alba succumbed on a frigid February day, during an intense blizzard with near-whiteout conditions. Alison had somehow gotten her to the v-e-t wrapped in Alba's favorite blue blanket. When the v-e-t arrived, it took only one look at his face for Alison to know that it was time to let Alba go.

But she could not let Alba go! Some days, she could barely climb out of bed. It was weeks before she returned to the park where Alba used to take Alison for walks. Alison told me she thought of it as a test to see if she could go places that sparked memories of Alba—which was really everyplace. She had been here with Alba, and here and here. The Italian restaurant with twisty noodles down the block. The lobby of the building where she lived, where she and Alba went downstairs to pick up the mail. She now saw the world through Alba-colored glasses. And the park—oh, the park! Just one big jumble of Alba memories! Alba had walked Alison in the park so many times, because Alison needed to be walked at least a couple of times a day. Although it was a great responsibility, Alba was up to it. Poodles are very loyal that way.

The park was directly across the street, a block away from where Alison lived in a building so tall that they called it a high-rise and required dogs and their people to ride up and down in a large, noisy box called an elevator. An elevator is a box where humans try very hard not to look each other in the eye, because this was New York City, where no one looks each other in the eye, just like in the animal kingdom. Staring directly is considered a challenge.

"There are too many people here," Alison explained to me. "We do this to give each other space."

Space? There is not much space in a mechanical box that moves up and down, so I didn't know what she was talking about. My Alison, alas, can get very confused and is not the sharpest claw in the paw, but I grew to love her anyway.

In the park, there was a children's playground where the shorter humans fearlessly climbed the monkey bars, shouting, "Look at me! Look at this!" to their mothers and fathers and nannies on the sidelines. The mothers and fathers and nannies had forgotten how to play, because that's what happens to humans when they get taller, so all they did was yap. Yap, yap, yap. They had become too stiff to play-bow, and they ate their treats out of bags without having to perform tricks first. I'll never understand humans.

In the children's playground, there was a little section with swings. The ones for toddlers had plastic bucket seats, and the ones for taller humans had metal plates to sit on. The taller humans tirelessly pushed the smaller ones and made odd sounds, like "Whee!" Alison had longed to go with Alba on one of the plank swings, but she never got around to it. Partly, she was embarrassed because she thought it was really only for children, and she was afraid to look silly. She said she always regretted not going on the swing with Alba. I was like, why didn't you just do it? But I get it. Alison, like the moms and dads and nannies by the monkey bars, had forgotten how to play.

Tall Pin oak trees lined Riverside Park, along with an abundance of wooden benches where you could look out over the Hudson River. It was a very picturesque area and had brought Alison a lot of pleasure. Now, though, everything there reminded her that Alba was over the Rainbow Bridge. Instead of remembering how the two of them would sit on a perfectly chosen bench beneath a sprawling honey locust tree, listening to the laughter and happy cries of the short, boisterous humans over in the children's playground, she saw only a lonely bench sitting in the barren wasteland that was now her life. Instead of remembering how she would count the forty-nine steps down a stone staircase when Alba took her on one of their longer walks, she saw the cold, gray steps to an eternal, Alba-less hell. Oh, that Alison! Someone needs to lick her face.

When Alison finally returned to the park without Alba, she watched with longing as other dogs walked their humans, prancing along or pulling at their leashes because their humans were so poky. She wasn't sure she was up to petting a dog that was not Alba, but when a big and cheery golden retriever tried to jump up on her, hoping to get a pet, Alison relented and touched the animal's thick, soft fur. Alison buried her face in the fur and started to sniffle.

"I'm so sorry. My dog just passed away a few weeks ago, and it's still raw," Alison apologized.

"I get it," said the dog's person. "When I lost my first, I had a terrible time. Come to think of it, it doesn't get easier."

Petting the non-Alba dog did not kill Alison after all, so when a black-and-white cockapoo stopped to nuzzle her leg, Alison reached down instinctively.

"Oh, I'm sorry, may I?" Alison asked the dog's person, but her hand had already gravitated through sense memory to that special place behind the pup's ear.

She braced herself for a major breakdown, a grief fest, but the soft, plush feel of the dog's coat, the silky curls, and the quickening of Alison's pulse gave her a sudden insight: this was what she was missing! She would have to get another puppy.

Months earlier, a poodle breeder named Agnes had friended her online, so Alison raced home to look up the breeder's profile. All of Agnes's dogs looked healthy and happy, and she had a slew of five-star reviews from satisfied humans. Alison fired off a text to the breeder, asking if she was going to have a litter anytime soon and explaining her terrible grief over the loss of her beloved Alba.

"I'm only interested in a black female," Alison typed.

"I suppose it's possible," the breeder typed back, "but most of my pups are chocolate."

"No, I definitely don't want that. My Alba was chocolate."

"I'm not a crystal ball."

This Agnes sounded a little crabby, even in her texts.

"And she has to be healthy," Alison messaged.

"*All* my pups are healthy."

"When is the next litter due?"

"End of March."

Alison did the math, which was not hard—the end of March was only a month away! That was hardly any time at all, considering the panic and anxiety and second thoughts and night sweats that Alison would need to pack in before actually picking up that puppy.

A few weeks passed, and Alison was jumping out of her skin.

"Hi, Agnes. It's Alison again. I just want to know how things are going with the puppies."

"I KNOW WHO YOU ARE" Agnes typed back. "Nothing new to tell you from two minutes ago."

A few days after that: "Hi, it's Alison again. . . . How is the mama poodle doing?"

Half a day went by before Agnes texted back: "I'll let you know WHEN I KNOW."

Alison's friend Michael, an architect she used to date, but with whom she'd remained close, took her out on her birthday, April 2.

"Do you think the mama poodle is okay? Because the breeder said the end of March, and it's already April . . ."

"Hon, come on, we're gonna toast to your birthday," said Michael. The waiter had brought them two glasses of pinot noir, and Alison and Michael clinked glasses. "To you, honey. You're going to have a great year."

"What if no black female is born?" said Alison before the glass even touched her lips. "Maybe it's too soon anyway for another dog."

9

Michael sighed. "You're just going to have to wait and see."

Alison hardly tasted her salmon as she continued to check her phone for messages. "Do you think maybe something's wrong?" she asked Michael, whose attempts at non-puppy conversation had gone nowhere.

It wasn't until Alison was home and getting ready for bed that the first message came in from the breeder. The dam had begun to whelp.

"Chocolate male," Agnes texted.

Oh no, thought Alison. Please, please, not chocolate. I cannot look at a chocolate poodle and not think about Alba.

Half an hour later, another chocolate male.

A few minutes passed and a third chocolate male arrived, although the breeder thought this puppy might be too frail to survive. "One more to go," she texted.

Alison knew that yoga breathing was a very handy thing during a stressful time like this, so she breathed in deeply . . . and then forgot all about yoga breathing and went back to hyperventilating, which was easier and more familiar. Anxiety was her wheelhouse.

Then, at 11:20 p.m., Alison received the final message of the night. Despite the late hour, she just knew that Michael would enjoy being roused from bed for this exciting news.

"Huh?" said Michael when she called him, sounding totally asleep.

"Michael, Michael, Michael!" Alison said with all the comportment she could muster. "Guess what? A black female was just born! And on my birthday! It's a sign!"

"It's a sign you're nutty," Michael said with a slightly grumpy voice. "Hon, I'm happy for you, but why don't you just go to bed now and let me go to bed, too."

Six weeks later, Michael drove Alison about an hour away to New Jersey, where the breeder lived. She fidgeted with the radio the entire way.

"Honey, I can't take any more Bee Gees. Could you look at the map so we can find this place?" asked Michael.

"What do you think she'll be like?" asked Alison.

"She'll be special. Are we on the right road?"

"Different from Alba, right?"

"Alison, focus!" exclaimed Michael, turning down the radio volume.

Once they found the large, beat-up-looking two-story house in West Milford, they rang the bell and heard an immediate siren of barking dogs. An elderly heavyset woman in a flowing smock answered the door.

"Hi, Agnes. I'm Alison . . ."

"Fer cryin' out loud, you think I don't know that? You are too much," said Agnes. "Wait over there on the couch."

The designated couch was cluttered with towels and newspapers. On the coffee table, Alison almost knocked over one of the many trophies with Agnes's name on it, along with her winning dog. There were photographs and blue ribbons on the walls with all of Agnes's prize-winning poodles from over the years.

"At least she really does breed poodles," Alison whispered to Michael. "That has to be a good sign, right?"

"Do you think she lured you here under false pretenses to sell you a schnauzer?"

"Stranger things have happened."

Agnes came into the room holding a black poodle, but Alison was confused.

"Um, is that the new puppy? It looks a bit . . . older," said Alison, treading carefully for fear the breeder was a bit psycho.

"Don't be ridiculous, this is my Chloe," said Agnes as she plopped herself down on a chair, the elderly poodle on her lap. "Well, what do you think? Do you want the puppy or not?"

Alison exchanged a brief look with Michael. He seemed to be suppressing a giggle.

"Well, yes, I think so," said Alison. "But perhaps I can meet her first?"

"Listen, you, I have a waiting list for my dogs. I know city people think you can have whatever you want, but you need to tell me right away if you want her or I'm moving on to the next taker."

"No, don't do that!" said Alison. "It's just . . . can you bring her out with her two brothers? I'd love to see them all together."

"The two chocolates are already sold."

"Yes, yes," said Alison in her most reassuring tone. "I just want to see them together. There's nothing so joyous like seeing puppies romp around, right?"

Agnes grimaced, clearly at war with herself over whether to maintain her haughty saleslady face or melt at the shared obsession with all things puppies.

"Okay, I'll bring them out. Fair warning, though. The girl is needy. She was the only one that cried when I left them. Do you work in an office? Because it's better for this one if you're home a lot."

"Yes, I'm home a lot," said Alison.

Agnes grunted and made a big show of getting up from her chair, as if Alison had asked her to climb Everest instead of going to the next room, but soon, the two male puppies came running and tumbling through the door. They came right over to the couch to get a good look at the two new humans. They nuzzled Alison's leg.

"It's like they know you need a puppy," said Michael. He had gone with Alison when she first got Alba, back when they were still a couple, and had helped with puppy training.

The two puppies started running all over the room until they ended up beneath the chair where Agnes had again taken a seat with her ancient dog in her lap.

Drum roll, please—because this is where I made my first entrance. I was a mighty black beauty, even though I was only a pound and a half, and I had a pink bow that perfectly offset the silky black of my hair. I kept a little distance from the new humans because, really, who *were* these two and why was one of them making squeaky cooing sounds of delight?

"Can I put her on my lap?" asked Alison.

"Be my guest," said Agnes in a tone that didn't sound as hospitable as her words.

Alison picked me up in her arms and held me to her chest. She squeezed me like she was going to flatten me out. Hey, take it easy!

"Oh, little girl," said Alison. "I'm Alison. I'm so pleased to meet you. Am I going to be your new forever person? Your new mama?"

And then she did something that was very curious. It was the first time I saw her face leak. Later, I would see it all the time, but this was new to me and a little strange. I felt droplets of water plink onto my beautiful black coat. I hoped this lady was not going to keep leaking like that.

Wow, her chest was beating so fast.

"Michael, she's so quiet," said Alison, wiping up the leak with the back of her hand. "Do you think she'll have a personality like her brothers?"

Whoa, I have plenty of personality! Oodles of poodle personality! How could she not see that?

"Just give her time. She's a baby," said Michael.

At least the other human seemed to get it. What did this Alison person expect? I was six weeks old. I had barely met any other humans except for the lady with the intriguing odor on her fingers and the children who kept waking me from my naps.

Alison kept squeezing me against her chest. It felt good and safe, but it also felt a little tight. I needed to get it across to her that she didn't have to squeeze that hard.

I knew just what to do—I kissed her nose.

"Well, do you want her?" asked the breeder impatiently.

"Yes, yes, I want her," said Alison. "Now my life will be happy."

I have to admit, I was beginning to feel the same way.

Monkey Girl

"Hon, any name yet?" asked Michael as he drove us to the city where I would begin my new life.

"I have a thing for Italian names," said Alison. "Alba means the dawn or sunrise in Italian, but I need a different Italian name for this little ball of intense cuteness."

I knew she was talking about me, partly because she said that last part in a very high, unnatural voice while sticking her face into mine.

"What about Bella?" suggested Michael.

"Way too common. Maybe Dolce? Or Luna?"

"She's got that jet-black coloring. How about Licorice?"

I could see Alison give the man a really strange look, like she was going to strangle him.

"That's not Italian," she said in a very stern voice, "and I'm not naming her after candy." I had heard that stern tone before. The woman with the nice-smelling fingers used it when I missed the wee-wee pad.

"Don't they have anisette liqueur over there?" said Michael. "Isn't that kind of the same thing?"

Alison still had that stare going on, and I hoped Michael would find the right wee-wee pad really soon or there was going to be trouble.

"She's very regal," said Michael. "You can call her Principessa."

Alison twisted me this way and that as she peered at different parts of me. Did she think my name was written on my paws?

"You're right, she's quite regal. Like a goddess," said Alison. "What about Dea? It means goddess. It's higher than a princess. It's the highest of all."

Then her voice changed again into the high-pitched one, the way those short humans sounded when they squealed at my antics. "Hi, Dea! That's your name! That's your name!" said Alison at a frequency I think only dogs can hear. "Do you like it?"

What in the world was she yapping about? I licked her nose to knock some sense into her.

"Look, I think she likes it," Alison said in her normal voice as she stroked me behind my ears.

Oops, I'm feeling a little woozy. This Michael does not know how to drive, and everything is starting to swim in front of my beautiful dark, expressive oval eyes. I know they are beautiful and dark and oval and all that because Alison already said so at least twice since we've been in this roller coaster of a car.

Oops, I think I need to throw up. I can't help it. This is my first car ride, and Michael is a terrible driver, and this lady Alison is new, and I'm about to see my forever home, and it's all just a little too much for me.

Ahh, that's better now!

When we arrived at the place where Alison said I was going to live, she carried me in my comfy bag into a big box that made noise—"This is the elevator," Alison told me—and carried us up, up, up to a high floor. There was a hallway with a few doors, and then Alison opened one of them with her key, and here it was, my forever home!

It was very large, so much larger than my crate with the newspaper. I felt like my world had suddenly opened up. Thank goodness Alison showed me my green blanket that the lady with the delightfully smelly fingers had given me so I could snuggle with it whenever I wanted. I grabbed it with my teeth and dragged it with me as Alison showed me around. The blanket had protective properties, and I needed it very close by, just in case the world suddenly came to an end, which I believed was a real possibility.

You can never be too careful.

As Alison showed me room after room and gave each one a name, I saw the potential for a lot of places where I could play or run or hide. This was a very promising start! The "living room" had lots of what the breeder lady had called don't-jump-on-that furniture. That's an umbrella term for what is basically a collection of comfortable, plushy places to sit and maybe gnaw on things. These places also have big, soft pillows that are perfect for drooling on, nicely absorbent material. I was very pleased to see that Alison had so many pieces of don't-jump-on-that furniture.

But wait. Why was there something blocking off this part of my new home? It was a long, high, silver metal gate that stretched from one side of the living room wall to the other side near the kitchen. On each side of the gate was a large, heavy box, loaded with books to weigh it down, blocking the ends of the gate so no one could get inside, including me. What was that all about? I could see there were changes that would have to be made, according to my doggie sense of feng shui.

"Look at this, Dea," said Alison. "This is the kitchen!"

I don't know why she was so proud of the kitchen instead of the living room with the comfy cushions and drool-worthy pillows. This kitchen place was kind of bare. All I could see was a tall white box, very large, that made my nose cold when I headbutted it. Opposite the cold box were some other boxy white things. At the end of the kitchen was a crate for me like the one I had with the breeder lady, but this one had something soft inside to lie on, no yucky newspaper. I carried my green blanket into the crate for safekeeping before Alison tried to steal it away from me. She hadn't tried to yet, but I knew that once she realized the blanket's magical properties of protection, she might want it for herself. She seemed very nice and all, but I thought it was important to establish some boundaries right up front: this was my green blanket. It kept me safe. Go get your own, lady!

Oh, here was something I recognized—a wee-wee pad. I sniffed it and then did my first pee right in the center. Alison rushed in and nearly knocked me over with the gale force of her praise: "Oh, Dea, you are *such* a good girl! Yes, you *are*! Yes, you *are*!"

Yes, I am. It goes without saying.

Oh, and here's something else I recognized: a bowl. I dunked my face into it and lapped at the cold, shimmering water. It looked like I had just about everything I needed in life, except there was still that metal gate-like thing blocking me from relaxing in the living room, where I could chew and drool on all kinds of don't-jump-on-that furniture.

Whoa, what's this? Alison picked me up and brought me into yet *another* room. What has she got here, a palace? How many rooms do humans need? "Dea, this is the bedroom, and here is your nighttime crate, right next to my bed," she said. "And before we go to sleep, we can watch TV!"

She pointed to a wide box at the foot of the bed that suddenly came to life with moving pictures and noise. For a moment, I saw a puppy scoot by along the screen, but it showed no interest in playing with me, which was bizarre.

Let me see if I had this straight: at night she'd get the big bed with the comfy blanket and soft pillows, while I stayed on the floor in a crate? I think not! Why couldn't I stay on the big bed, too? It was becoming clear that Alison did not always think very clearly.

"My mom always felt dogs needed their own space to sleep," said Alison, almost as if hearing my thoughts, which was a good start toward the ESP I hoped she would pick up. I intended to send her thought waves about my hunger levels. "I grew up with that in my head, hearing my mom's voice saying dogs should not sleep in the bedroom, and never in the bed. But we'll see. Maybe if you're a good girl . . ."

What's with the "maybe?"

Next, we were back to the room with the wee-wee pad and the cold box.

"Dea, sweet girl, this is where you'll stay when I'm out," said Alison. "I won't always be able to take you with me, and I have a medical appointment tomorrow that I just can't change." She placed a star-shaped squeaky toy inside the crate and told me I was such a good girl. But if I'm such a good girl, what's with this crate in the kitchen? Why couldn't I be on the bed in the bedroom? Why couldn't I go to her appointment with the human v-e-t, too? She would hardly notice I was there, except for when I scratched or chased things or sniffed strangers or demanded petting. She would hardly notice at all.

The kitchen crate was not so bad, as crates went. I knew of two in my life, and this one was far preferable. It had a soft pillow and my green blanket with special powers of protection. Plus, when I nibbled on the star-shaped toy, it gave off a marvelous, blaring squeak. Let's just hear that again.

Oh, wait . . . what? What was she doing with this wooden gate thing that she just pulled out to block the kitchen door? Oh, no. Two gates now? That will not do. I hate confinement. This just will not work. Take me back to the breeder.

"Yes, it fits okay for when I go out tomorrow, sweet girl," said Alison as if I was supposed to applaud this terrible turn of events.

The first night, I slept in my bedroom crate on the floor like I was supposed to, but I had terrible nightmares of wooden gates closing and hoppity rabbits that eluded my grasp. The world was bleak. I would have to train Alison that my place was in the bed, with her.

The next morning, Alison proved she had no end of surprises for me: She tied my ears back before breakfast.

"You look so adorable!" she squealed. "It looks like you've got a ponytail!"

She explained that this was so I wouldn't get food in my longish ears. Then she watched me eat my breakfast, the same yucky food from the breeder that was not quite as tasty as I believed I deserved, after which she announced that she was going to close the crate door to keep me safe in the wee-wee pad room. She stretched out the smaller wooden gate that blocked the kitchen doorway. She had a nerve! I was in prison, probably for life, incarcerated, and for what reason I did not know. Had I not been a *good girl*? Why this terrible punishment?

Alone. Abandoned.

"I'll be back soon," she lied to me.

Soon? What does that word even mean? She had left me forever. Forever and a day.

I let out an existential howl of despair that had the desired effect—Alison came running back into the kitchen with a look of concern.

"Okay, Dea, I'll keep the crate door unlocked so you can snuggle inside or come out into the kitchen if you want. The gate will keep you safe inside the kitchen."

Honestly, I was surprised I had won this first battle so easily. I was eager to try my luck pushing more boundaries in the future.

The minute Alison was gone, I didn't even have to tap my innate intelligence because all I needed to do was push my nose against the crate door to open it. I had made it past the first of the three obstacles that stood in my way of chewing, drooling, and other necessary aspects of total freedom.

I surveyed my next foe—the wooden kitchen door gate. I triangulated its height and considered my options. It was time to make the great escape. I had never jumped before, but I am a poodle after all and quite athletic. The breeder lady had said poodles are like circus dogs, able to do all sorts of tricks. Now was the perfect time to test her theory.

I gulped some water from the bowl to fortify myself before revving up and charging. I sailed right over the gate! My paws slid along the shiny wooden floor on the other side and came to a halt in the big, wide world of freedom. Triumph.

Now it was time to roll up my sleeves, even though I do not have any sleeves and would not know how to roll them, and get to work. I had a lot to do before Alison came home. I needed to try and get past the bigger metal gate and thus get inside the living room with all its comfy wonders. Were the throw pillows sufficiently soft? I couldn't wait to test them, but something closer at hand demanded my attention. Alison had thoughtfully left behind some rubber galoshes on a mat near the big door, no doubt so that I'd have something interesting to chew. She hadn't left any other toys around, so the rubber galoshes would have to do. Note to self: Set Alison straight.

I had fallen into a deep slumber by the time I heard Alison's key in the lock. I was lying by the front door in the middle of a lovely *squirrel* dream, but I jumped up at the sound of her voice calling me and made a point to welcome her home, my nonstop wagging tail swinging in a flutter.

"*Dea*! How did you get out of the kitchen?" she squealed. "What did you do?"

It was easy enough, I wanted to boast—but she didn't actually sound all that happy with my acrobatic feat.

"What am I going to do with you, you little monkey girl," she said.

I am ashamed to admit I was wrong about Alison. She is *not* as slow and obtuse as the other humans of my acquaintance. She picked up right away that I did not want to be enclosed and she began keeping my crate door open, except at night when we slept. Any question who's the boss here? I have already trained her well.

And, come on, my needs were few. All I needed was food, water, treats, toys, scratches, pets, exercise, attention, *more* attention, and always to be extremely near Alison every moment of the day and night. *All the time.*

That was not too much to ask, in my opinion.

But, what's this? "Dea, I need to go out again for a bit. Forgot to pick up milk for my coffee," said Alison. "Be a good monkey girl." Oh, no, not again! Please don't go. I beg of you. I'll be a good monkey girl.

Ignoring my pleas, she left. The door closed behind her.

It was doubly bad because Alison knew very well how I felt about being left alone. She had already confided to me that she knew the feeling and had even felt it herself.

Alison's mother had been the only parent she really had after her parents divorced. Alison lived with her mother while her older brother, David, and older sister, Deane, stayed with their father, a handsome man with a mov- ie-star smile who worked in the advertising business. He was good at selling ideas, but he sold Alison short, in Alison's view. He said he would be there for her, but it wasn't true. "A father is supposed to protect a child," she told me. "But mine completely severed my family. A sharp knife wouldn't have done so much harm."

Alison never understood why her father separated her from her siblings when she was six years old. She grew up feeling isolated and alone from an early age. Neither parent ever told her the real reason, and it left her with an indelible sensation of rejection. How could she trust her own worth if her father had left her behind?

She was not altogether unhappy staying with her mother, but she knew that if one parent didn't want her, nothing was off the table. Alison loved and revered her mom, but she felt she had to keep proving that she was a good daughter and worth keeping. She tried to make her mother proud by getting top grades and honing perfectionistic behavior, like sending out thank-you notes for gifts she had barely opened.

At times, Alison and her mother butted heads, especially over how

Alison wanted more time with her, just the two of them. But her mother remarried a bookstore owner named George and said a terrible thing: "He's the love of my life," she said.

That made Alison uneasy. Did it mean her mother had never loved Alison's father? Was Alison not created in love? Was she an unwanted baby?

Whenever Alison argued with her mother, she became penitent and couldn't apologize enough. She went way overboard in the opposite direction out of fear she had caused an irreparable rift and soon no one would want her at all. She would dash out to the neighborhood florist and use allowance money to buy her mother daisies along with baby's breath. "Oh, sweet girl, you're the best," her mom would say. "George will love this too."

Back in her mother's good graces, Alison got the oxygen she needed, but she always had to share it with George.

Meanwhile, she had adored her brother, David, who was ill for most of his life after a diagnosis of Crohn's disease at the age of eleven. He was always an altruistic sort, never focusing on his own needs. He always managed to turn the conversation around to the other person.

When they were older, he lived in Florida, just an hour and a half away from their mother, so Alison could see both of them when she visited. No matter how ill he felt, he would make time for her. He sent her loving cards for her birthday that told her he felt fortunate to have her as his sister. He was more like a doting father figure than her own father, who died at the early age of fifty-seven. David was one of the few people who knew Alison well enough to see the sadness in her eyes, maybe because there was a sorrow in his own beautiful blue-gray eyes. He hid it with a million-dollar smile, but that didn't fool Alison.

He was forever available to her. When she had boyfriend troubles, David was the person she could call. He would say, "I love you completely."

She loved him completely, too, but it was bittersweet because he'd been ill for so long that there was always the threat of losing him. The thought of it caused an ache in Alison so profound that she disappeared into denial. It was a coping technique she would need many times again in her life: She decided David would live forever and always be there for her. The alternative was unthinkable.

David died when he was sixty-three from complications of his illness. Their mother died a year and a half later, and Alison worried that the stress of losing her son had contributed to it. "No parent should have to bury their child," she said.

With David gone, Alison could barely move from her bed. She kept the television on just for noise but couldn't focus on anything.

Out of the gloom of these deaths came Grace, Alison's father's aptly named first cousin—a quirky octogenarian who got back in touch to see how Alison was doing with all that loss. It made Alison feel safe and loved again.

Grace had a voice that was light and airy, like it was flowing in the wind. Even over the phone, Alison could hear the smile in that voice. More important, Grace understood Alison's pain and didn't judge her for it.

Little by little, Alison tried to move forward. She even began to date again. She would tell Grace about each new man and ask her opinion. Sometimes, Grace would laugh her infectious laugh and they would both howl together as they assessed each date's potential: "He looks like he's hiding something. Maybe he's with the FBI!"

Grace was also an animal lover. She fed the birds outside her home in Virginia when it was cold out and had many cherished dog companions in her life. Alison would send her beautiful photos of Alba after a trip to the groomer and sign the messages from Alba. Grace would write back: "You belong on the cover of *Doggie Vogue*!"

Grace was a glass-half-full person to Alison's half-empty one. Gradually, Alison's glass began to fill. She felt a sense of family again. Her feeling of well-being when Grace was around was magical—but just as with her beloved brother, Alison had a hard time escaping the fear that this wonderful, safe feeling might not last.

It didn't. Grace died a few years after they reunited. Alison lost her best friend, although she still sometimes heard Grace's magical voice urging her onward with her life.

That's how I knew Alison would never stay mad with me for long, because she knew what I was going through. "It's separation anxiety," she told me. "It's a killer."

Well, *that* did not make me feel any better! If it's a "killer," would I die from it? I certainly felt as if I might!

Thanks to a few rearrangements in the household, I could now be in the wee-wee pad room *and* in part of the living room, although another part remained sectioned off so I wouldn't jump on the don't-jump-on-that furniture. I had my freedom, but I didn't have my human. I cried and moaned and yelped, which only made me want to take a nap.

In my sleep, I saw that *squirrel* again. He wanted me to chase him. I flailed my paws in the air. My nose and ears twitched.

After my nap, I sniffed around for something to do. A chew toy, perhaps? But Alison had only left me a nylon bone and a few hard toys. I needed to chew something a little mouthier. Ahh, I found the perfect thing—a long, chewable strip of wood along the base of the wall where it met the floor. It had lots of natural corners. It's not that it tasted so good, but it felt soothing to nibble with my dagger-like baby teeth. I went to work and made sure I gnawed each corner uniformly and left the wood damp with my saliva. Good monkey girl!

"Dea, I'm home," Alison announced when she returned. Then she made a sharp intake of breath before yelling: "What did you do?"

What a drama queen. Can she not see how much dedicated dental work I put into this? How I made sure it was all so evenly munched?

"Dea, you chewed all my baseboards!"

And the problem with that is . . . what, exactly?

She peered inside my mouth like she was searching for lost housekeys, running her fingertip over my little knife-like teeth. "Good, they're all still here," she said.

Next, she moved my crate from the wee-wee pad room into the big room, but only within a sectioned-off area. She shut me inside the crate. Who can understand these humans?

Finally, she picked up a plastic box with a cord dangling out of one end and talked at it.

"Hello, is this Bev, the behaviorist?" she said to the plastic thing. "Stan and Arthur in my building recommended you. I need help with my new puppy. She suffers from separation anxiety, and she just chewed up all my baseboards. I'm feeling overwhelmed, and I just don't know what to do. Can you please come here right away?"

Training Alison

T he first thing Bev the behaviorist did was to solve the mystery that had plagued me all my young life. When she came in the door, she reached into a small bag and brought out something that smelled familiar. She held it out and I chomped on it, and that's when I put two and two together and got—*cheese*! So, *this* was the pungent odor that was always on the fingers of the breeder. It was a double-header of delight: a mystery solved and a mouthful of *cheese*.

This lady was a true find. She picked me up and held me in her arms, not too tightly. She gave me a kiss on my face. "Hello, little Dea. You're such a good girl," she said. I am so special that even this lady knows it. I give off an aura of specialness and fan it far and wide with my tail.

She took me into the kitchen where the wee-wee pad was and sat on the floor, holding me in her lap.

"Wait, are you giving her cheese?" asked Alison. "Is that okay for a puppy?"

"Of course," said Bev. "Don't you know what a high-end treat is?"

"Well, I guess not."

Bev gave an exaggerated sigh. "Oh, Alison," she said.

Bev the behaviorist fed me pieces of kibble, although hope sprang eternal, and I trusted that eventually she would go back to the *cheese*.

"I don't understand," Alison was saying. "What am I doing wrong?"

"Everything."

"What is that supposed to mean?"

"Listen, you need to give little Dea more treats. She's so sweet and good," said Bev. Oh, how I like this woman. "Also, you need to get her a KONG. It's a plastic container you can fill with frozen nonfat yogurt, plus a little peanut butter and banana. Freeze it and she'll be busy with that and stop her crying."

"KONG," repeated Alison. "Okay, I didn't know."

"How can you not know these things? Never mind. What else have you done to train her?"

"I haven't had time to train her," said Alison. "I can barely leave her, even for an hour. She just cries and cries."

"You need to read my book on how to train a puppy. I have an extra copy in my bag I can sell you."

"Look, I'm trying . . ."

"*I'll* say," said Bev.

Alison began to get the wet face again. I wondered why. She had so many v-e-t appointments; maybe she should ask one of them about this.

Once Alison's face continued to leak, things turned sour and she made Bev the behaviorist leave, just when it was my very last chance *ever* to have more *cheese*. Life can be so unfair.

But life can also be wonderful—and it certainly was when, the next moment, my ears puffed up at the sound of the clinking leash. We're going out! The clinking leash was the signal that I was going to walk Alison. She needed plenty of walks, and I was happy to oblige. I did it so well that sometimes she gave me a peanut butter treat.

As soon as we got outside, I yanked her with all my might toward the park. "Dea, stop pulling," she said.

Why would she say that? The wind was blowing in my direction, sending all kinds of delicious scents my way. My destiny was calling. I was still a little puppy but mighty strong in the shoulders.

I zigzagged all over the street as I tried to keep up with the new smells. "Dea, stop *pulling!*" Alison said again.

Alison needs to be walked so often because of an incident a long time ago when she was in high school and Natasha, her poodle, was supposed to walk her. One day after school, she lied to her mother and said Natasha had walked her. But her mother got the real lowdown from the doorman and was furious. From then on, Alison was very docile about letting poodles take her for a walk, even when it's raining out. But she does get a little sluggish sometimes and doesn't want me pulling on the leash, even though she is wrong and I am right.

Let me put it another way: I am right and she is wrong.

It's not Alison's fault that she's so slow to understand some things. In my vast experience, humans are not playing with a full jar of peanut butter. They're just made that way. And explaining it goes nowhere—I can bark and bark, and she'll still say, "What's the matter? What's wrong? Does something hurt?"

Sheesh, these people.

At the entrance to the park, I tugged Alison down the ramp instead of waiting for her to count out all forty-nine steps. At the bottom was Shangri-la—furry *squirrels* with big eyes, clutching snacks in their tiny claws. Their long, curly tails beckoned me. Clearly, they wanted me to chase them. They raced up the tall trees and I tried to follow, but Alison, spoilsport that she is, wouldn't let me.

I saw birds flying over me and heard a sweet chirping from somewhere up above. The world was thrumming with life and creatures that begged to be chased.

Our walks so far had been delicate little things, but now I found myself stepping upon something new and heavenly—it was green and springy and dense. It felt like velvet and had an intoxicating perfume. I rolled and rolled in it.

"Dea, we can't go on the grass here, there's a sign," said Alison. "I'll find another place where it's okay to do that."

I scurried around, marking my territory as I went. It is *all* my territory, actually, but I must leave something behind to remind others.

"Good girl, monkey," said Alison, giving me two peanut butter treats and a sweet pat beneath my chin. My Alison is a treasure.

When we came to the ramp leading back up to the sidewalk, I put my powerful shoulders into it, dragging Alison forward. I am the natural leader of this pack.

"Dea, stop pulling!" she said.

Doesn't she see that I need to be in the lead? It is in my nature. No way is it in *her* nature. How can I get this across to her?

To finish off the most enjoyable walk of my life—there haven't been that many so far, but this one was by far the best—I spotted Jackson. Do poodles blush? Maybe. Jackson is a golden-colored Havanese puppy who lives in our building with her guys, Stan and Arthur, who knew Bev the behaviorist.

Jackson saw me coming and our tails began to wag in unison, lightning-fast metronomes. We are not like those silly humans who dare not express their affection until their lawyers have signed off on all the documents. Jackson and I rolled and tumbled all over each other and nibbled each other's ears. While Alison exchanged polite nonsense with Stan and Arthur, my puppy energy burned brightly for Jackson. As a further sign of our happiness, we intertwined our leashes once, twice, who knows how many times! Perhaps it was a world record. It took Alison and the guys quite a while to untangle them while Alison muttered some not-very-hospitable things.

When we got back home, Alison reached for that plastic box with a cord and talked at it for a long time. An eternity of paying attention to a box and not to me. She was in the living room inside the gate that kept me outside of her space, sectioned off, so I explored where I could and found the corner of a woolly covering on the floor. It begged to be nibbled. Although it wasn't like real food, it did have a very satisfying texture.

"Dea, what are you doing?" Alison screamed. "Oh, my God, Dea. You ate part of my rug?"

While Alison rushed to pet the chewed rug instead of petting gorgeous me, I grabbed my loudest squeaky toy and began to squeak it, looking straight at Alison with complete defiance. I have a sound I like to use along with that look, a high-pitched bark, kind of like a monkey screeching. This is my way of saying I am going to do what I want to do, which sounds very reasonable to me, but when my bark descended into more of a growl, it surprised even me. What a great sound I was producing! Very masterful.

"Dea, what's wrong with you?" said Alison. "You're acting like a devil dog!"

She reached again for the plastic thing with the cord and started talking to it. She certainly likes to talk to plastic boxes.

"I need to bring her in," she told the box. "She just ate part of my area rug."

By the time we got to the big building full of people in white coats, I had tossed up that piece of woolly rug I had eaten. The nice man in the white coat felt my belly and poked me all over. He opened my mouth and looked at my teeth. What on earth was he looking for in there? But he didn't hurt me.

"She'll be fine, but I suggest you move that rug," he announced.

On the way home, I knew Alison was upset with me but in all honesty, I couldn't figure out why. She should have been grateful I busied myself with chewing instead of whimpering, which I already knew she didn't like.

Then she said something terrible.

"Dea, it's not working out. Maybe it was too soon to get another puppy."

As soon as she said those words, her face began to leak.

After that, Alison was in a bad mood and slow with the dinner. She had gotten rid of the nasty stuff the breeder lady used to give me, and I was really hankering for my yummy new chicken-and-brown-rice kibble. I squeaked my green elephant squeaky toy—it made a marvelous shrill sound—to remind her it was time for me to chow down, but she had locked herself in the bedroom and I could hear her talking, probably to that stupid box again.

When she emerged from her room, she seemed calmer. Talking to the box seemed to have helped.

"Dea, my sweet girl, my monkey girl, it's all going to work out," she said. "Sheila is coming."

Sheila? Is that a type of food?

A few days later, a tall woman came through the door. I liked her right away because she let me pull her long, flowing hair.

"Dea, stop. Leave Sheila alone," said Alison, but the new lady claimed it was okay.

"Just let her be," said this Sheila person.

She put me on her lap, clearly to encourage me to nibble the buttons on her shirt. Sheila didn't stop me, so Alison just looked on and stayed quiet. Alison's training was really starting to take hold!

"Please keep Dea's collar and this training leash on her at all times during her lessons," said Sheila. "When you give her a command and she does it correctly, give her a freeze-dried chicken treat. These are the only treats she's going to get from now on. They're very high-end, and she gets them only when she does something you ask her to do."

"Got it."

See how easy it is when your human is in the hands of a good trainer?

"I want you to ask Dea to just sit and stay with the training leash on," Sheila continued. "Push her little behind down on the ground to help guide her."

"Dea, sit! Sit! Good girl," said Alison. "That was the one thing we already worked on."

"Good. Give her a treat right away. Now ask her to sit and then stay. Put your hand out like this." Sheila showed Alison how to flex her hand in an upward position for "stay."

"Dea, sit! Stay!" said Alison.

Whoa there! First, she wants me to sit, and then she wants me to stay? The woman cannot make up her mind. A better use of my time is to pull on Sheila's buttons again.

"Don't give her too many commands at once," said Sheila. "Keep trying every day for about five minutes. Puppies don't have long attention spans. Here, I've written it all out for you, everything you need to do with Dea. The good news is poodles are quick learners."

For the next few days, Alison attached my training leash to my collar, and we repeated Sheila's commands.

"One more time, Dea, come on. Sit," said Alison. "Good girl! Good girl!" She gave me a freeze-dried chicken treat right away. I was liking this new plan.

She moved a few feet away and put her hand up. "Dea, stay," she said.

If I did that, would I get another chicken treat? Yes, I would! I am a bit of a clairvoyant, it turned out.

Just like that, our lives began to change for the better. Alison no longer called me a devil dog, and I began to do things that forced her to give me special treats.

The only dark lining to this cloud is that I still couldn't stand to be alone. It's in my DNA, I think. It makes me feel abandoned and unsafe. Michael said Alison and I are two peas in a pod, but that's silly, because I am a poodle, not a pea. Another sad example of a clueless human. He wasn't a good driver, and he couldn't tell a poodle from a pea.

Now, whenever Alison came back after leaving me until the end of time—which she still did, like whenever she went to the gym—she hugged me fiercely and kissed me on the cheek while I licked hers all over. There is always a nice salty flavor there, especially after she leaks, so I was doing her a favor by licking it off. When she buried her face in me and said, "I love you, Dea," it was so muffled I could barely make out what she was saying, but at least I was sure that she was an essential part of my pack. She and I would be together forever.

The Bald Guy with the Cap

While Alison was getting my dinner ready, I detected something that smelled nearly as enticing as the food—she had left a pair of leather boats with sticks on the end outside our bedroom door. I had never seen anything like these before and needed to investigate with my nose. I like to poke my snout into things and inhale and let the computer part of my doggie brain compute the hundreds of things that make a scent very particular, very soul-enriching, like no other in the world.

Whatever these two leather boats with sticks were, my nose approved.

Poodles are, if nothing else, very into the scientific method. After my nose approved, it was time to find out what these things tasted like, which was the next logical step. I was feeling a bit peckish, after all, since Alison was being shamefully slow getting dinner into my bowl.

Oh, tasty! These things were great! Very nice mouth feel, kudos to the chef. The texture was perfect for that new set of teeth that was coming in. I hardly had time to nibble before Alison noticed my mouth moving.

"What do you have there, Dea? Are you chewing on something?"

Hmm? I looked up at her with my disarming look, although it was hard to keep my eyes from darting guiltily back and forth to the tasty tidbits.

"No, Dea! Bad girl! You're eating my shoes!" cried Alison. "Oh, look at that. My new pair of heels."

Bad? Did she say I was a bad girl? My life was over. And to think I was just peaking.

Sheila had told Alison to lower her voice and sound disappointed and stern if she caught me doing something wrong, but honestly, how could this be bad?

My scientific poodle brain reviewed every bit of the incident to try to puzzle it out.

1. Dinner did not arrive in a timely fashion.
2. Alison left these two leather things with sticks right next to my doughnut toy, meaning I should definitely chew on them.

I could not for the life of me see where I'd gone wrong.

I still got my dinner, but I gobbled it down twice as fast, just in case she got upset again for no reason and tried to take it away before I finished.

Surprisingly, she made no move to do so. Now that I thought of it, she wasn't even in the room with me anymore. She was doing something in our bedroom. Emanating from there was a sweet, cloying smell I did not appreciate in the least. It was way too strong. Not soul-enriching at all.

Wait, what was she doing? Was she getting ready to go somewhere without me? Did she give me my dinner as a ruse so she could sneak out and abandon me?

Was I still her monkey girl? I had to be her monkey girl.

She emerged from our bedroom wearing something different from usual. It was clothing that didn't have my scent securely embedded in it. And there was that terrible sweet smell on her neck; it was so nasty I didn't even want to lick it.

She uttered those words that were like a stake to my heart: "Monkey girl, I'm going out."

No, Alison, no! You are making a tragic mistake!

She gave me a kiss on the cheek, and I kissed her nose and inside her ear. Maybe that would stop her from leaving me. She laughed and said it tickled.

And then she walked out the big front door! Not a backward glance! Oh, the humanity.

My life was in tatters. I immediately grabbed my green blanket in my teeth. The green blanket kept me safe. I didn't know what I'd ever do without it.

I tried to pass some time chewing my Nylabone, but I kept wondering, "Lord, why?" My whimpering pleas went unanswered. There I was, alone in the vortex of hell.

Reluctantly, I decided to take a nap. I needed my rest so I could endure the long, cold, lonely nights ahead without Alison, who clearly had abandoned me for good.

Many seasons came and went until she walked back through the big front door and greeted me with a hug. She was no longer tense or upset about the leather boats with sticks and was even quite chatty. But where had she been? I sniffed around her for clues.

"I missed you, monkey girl," she said. Yay, I'm still her monkey girl! "I promised my friend Mary I would go to this sports event with her. Some player was getting an award. It was kind of boring but, well, something interesting happened!"

She told me about some guy—she said he was kind of cute. He was big and strong and had friendly brown eyes. He was bald but wore a baseball cap to hide it. "We talked, and before I left, he asked for my number."

This was not the first time I had heard about this incomprehensible ritual that humans have. They make up a bunch of numbers and hand them to each other on pieces of paper, or type them onto a small metal-and-glass rectangle every human is obliged to carry. I think it's the law that they have to carry one. And if a new version of the metal-and-glass rectangle comes out, it is important that everyone buy it for twice as much money as they paid for the last version.

So, they hand over this incomprehensible jumble of numbers, and if it's just two ordinary people, that's the end of that. But if it's two people who kind of like each other, they smile at each other goofily and agree to have lunch. I would think it's enough to know each other's name without asking for numbers as well. If it's that hard to remember who's who, they should wear ID tags on their collars so they won't get lost or confused.

"This guy that I met at the sports event, he wants to get together next weekend," said Alison. "You know what? I think I will."

Wait a minute, is this guy with the cap going to be a problem for me? I quickly did the math, because I am a very mathematical poodle, and if the two of them got together, what would happen to me? Who was this person who was going to take my Alison away from me? I would tear him apart with my mighty teeth, as soon as the new set came in!

When the time came for Alison to have dinner with this man from the sports event, she took a longer time than usual putting on clothing. I could also smell that same sweet, horrible smell on her neck. She told me she would be back "soon," but I didn't know what that meant. Whatever it was, "soon" was unacceptable. It was very close to a zillion years, and it was really too much to ask of me to wait by the door that long.

Only when Alison came home again, exactly a zillion years later, did I learn what she had been doing out there.

"Nice place, thanks for choosing it," she had said to the man, Ted. He had dressed casually in a blue button-down shirt and beige slacks and wore his baseball cap all during dinner. Maybe he was afraid his bald head would get cold from the blast of air conditioning.

"So, you were married, and then another relationship ended?" Alison prompted.

"Technically, I was only married once, but this last relationship was like a marriage, and I had another child with her," said Ted.

"Another?"

Alison caught the waiter's eye and asked for a glass of pinot noir. She felt she might need it.

"I have two kids," said Ted. "The older one is out of the house and on his own already, and my youngest, Lisa, is with me three or four nights a week."

Alison told me this man, Ted, came with some baggage, and I wondered whether it was the leather kind on the shoulder or the bigger kind with wheels. Alison did not specify. All dogs know that when they see your person take luggage out from the closet, it is very important to whine, cry, pitch a fit, and, if necessary, hurl themselves inside the bags so nothing can get packed in them.

"I play backgammon one night a week," he added. "How about you?"

"I'm not much of a game player," she said, doing the arithmetic in her head, even though my math skills were clearly superior. She figured he spent three or four nights a week with Lisa and another night for backgammon, which didn't leave a whole lot of nights for starting a new relationship.

After dinner this guy walked her home. "I had a really good time tonight, and I don't want it to end," said Ted.

Alison was surprised. She hadn't thought they had found much in common, but she did enjoy his company and didn't mind having a little more of it.

That's when she told him about me and went to get me. Yay! She's home! But when I took her downstairs in the noisy metal elevator box to the lobby for her walk, there was the guy, baseball cap and all. Would I have to walk him, too? That's a lot of responsibility for a puppy.

"This is Dea," she said. The man stroked my back. I supposed I could spare him a slight tail wag.

I walked the two of them around the block over and over while this Ted person kept yapping and Alison made odd, high-pitched giggling sounds while she paid absolutely no attention to me whatsoever. I did my business, so I was a good girl, but they still didn't take the hint. I thought I might have to keep walking them until it was time for Alison's morning walk.

Finally, thankfully, they said good night, and Alison and I went back home to our bedroom and snuggled. The stinky smell on her neck had worn off a little by then, so it was tolerable.

Alison and Ted began to see each other one night a week. After the second time out with him, she invited him upstairs into our home. She sat on a don't-jump-on-that sofa, and he sat on a don't-jump-on-that chair across from her. I was next to my Alison on the floor listening to them yap, a very boring conversation that never *once* touched upon the important things in life, like whether they enjoyed the sound squeaky toys make or how often to dispense treats to me (answer: very often). It was the same scenario again every week after that, her on the don't-jump-on-that sofa and him on a don't-jump-on-that chair—yap, yap, yap, no concern for *moi*. I don't know what Alison got out of these visits. She always acted nervous and strange when Ted was in the apartment. She kept her hands crossed tightly over her lap. Her voice changed, too. It went up a register, and she laughed her fool head off. Humans laugh their fool heads off over anything and nothing, in my poodle opinion, but it can get out of hand, and I feared Alison was in need of visiting a v-e-t.

Yes, Ted was a good petter, but he was an unnecessary addition to the living room. I tried to relay this to her by pawing her leg, but she didn't pay any attention.

Plus, whenever Ted was there, she was always petting me on top of my head, which was not my favorite place to be touched. Who needs a thump-thump-thump on the noggin? I really expected better from Alison by now.

Every time Ted left, he touched Alison's mouth with his for a moment. Maybe that was how humans sniffed each other? I hoped so, because from what I could see, humans failed woefully at sniffing each other. How could they possibly know each other without a good sniff? Humans seem ill-equipped for this world. I am surprised they have made it this far.

"Dea, I just don't know how I feel about him," Alison murmured to me. "He's very nice and makes time for me and loves dogs, but I just don't know if I'm attracted to him."

I knew what she meant. He was sort of nice to me, too, always petting me behind my ears and stroking my belly, but from my vast experience and my ability with math, there should not be an extra someone in the room. It should just be a dog and her person. One plus one equals perfect.

Alison did not heed my wisdom, and things really started to change, especially after one night when Alison went to a movie with Ted. It must have been an important movie because everything felt different afterward.

"That was fun, but I think it fell apart in the third act," Alison told Ted as they left the movie theater.

"Glad we had time to go see it before I go away," he said.

"Oh, you're going away?"

"It's our yearly summer break from the city. We go to New Hampshire every year."

"We?"

"My daughter and I meet my brother and his wife there," explained Ted.

"How long will you be gone?"

"About three weeks, give or take."

On the sidewalk in front of our building, they did their familiar peck on the lips good night. Alison came home to me and told me all about the movie—it sounded like a mess, with it falling apart in the third act and all—but she seemed to have a new attitude. I wasn't sure I liked it.

"He's going away for a long time," she said.

That was okay with me. I'd have her all to myself every night, no Ted taking up space in the living room and yap, yap, yapping.

Over the next few weeks, Alison and I practiced some more commands, like *give me paw* and *roll over*. There was a TV commercial she liked with a trainer showing a dog how to roll over, and she wanted to see if we could do that together. After two tries, I was a whiz and rolled over on command. Every time, I would get my favorite freeze-dried chicken treat.

"Dea, you're such a good girl. You're my monkey girl!"

Life was heaven. Except that Alison had been mentioning Ted's name a lot from the moment he left. That worried me. My mathematical wizardry said that she was mentioning "Ted" more times than "Dea," and that was all wrong. Wasn't I enough for her? Did one plus one equal zero all of a sudden?

"Dea, I wonder if Ted is thinking about us right now," she said.

It was the eternal mystery of humans—she hadn't felt much attraction to him until he went away, and now she wanted the thing she couldn't have. You'd never catch *me* acting like that, except that I needed my green blanket every time Alison so much as looked at the front door.

Two peas in a pod? Maybe Michael was onto something after all.

I could barely lie with my Alison and snuggle with her without hearing the man's name. Ted this, Ted that. Just when I thought she was about to rub my belly, she would sigh and say something about Ted and his strong arms.

"There's just something I can't get out of my mind, sweet girl," she said.

I looked at her with my limpid chocolate-brown eyes that were so dark, they almost looked black. Was it a treat for me that was on her mind? Was that what was occupying her thoughts, wondering when she would give me my next treat?

"I can't stop thinking about what it would be like to really kiss Ted."

Panting in the Bedroom

It took Alison longer than usual to get ready for dinner. She put some more of that disgustingly sweet smell on her neck, which she only seems to do before she sees Ted. I saw her spritz it there from a little jeweled glass bottle. Why would she want to stink like that? Is it her way of getting Ted out of our lives?

But I didn't want him out of our lives *too* quickly, because he had offered to cook dinner for Alison at his place, and this time, he invited me, too. I couldn't wait to sit at the table with them, just the three of us, with my ears tied back in my dinnertime ponytail look and maybe a napkin tied around my neck so I could sit upright on a chair with them. At least, this is how the scenario played out in my mind.

It's not exactly how it went down.

At first, things looked promising. It was only a short walk to Ted's apartment, where he greeted me first with a strong back rub. This was a man who had his priorities straight! His hands were sturdy. I felt protected when I was on his lap. He reminded me of a bulldog named Rufus I had recently sniffed in the park. Like Ted, the bulldog was big and robust. I liked sniffing him all over. Humans are shy and fastidious, so I only sniffed Ted on his face and chest. I left his butt alone. For some reason, humans bark at you when you try to sniff their butts.

But there were other smells that were just as enticing—whiffs of things that were new to me. Maybe some food would fall on the floor? Alison was a little too immaculate for my taste, always wiping up anything that dropped to the ground. Tiny bit of chicken? There was Alison like lightning, armed with a damp paper towel. I could barely get her to move fast enough when I took her for her walk, but if something delicious hit the floor, she was Johnny-on-the-spot. Just once I managed to snag a morsel of scrambled egg before she sprinted over with her Swiffer and microfiber cloths. The rich taste of the egg made me salivate long after that tidbit was gone.

Don't get me wrong—I was very happy with my chicken-and-brown-rice kibble and my chicken, peas, and potato canned food as long as I could also get my freeze-dried chicken treats, which Alison had taken to calling *cookies*. That word quickly became one of my favorites. It is a fine, fine word.

Well, this Ted was a gem, let me tell you. I had come out from under his bed, where I was coughing a little from the dust—I hoped Alison gave him a Swiffer and microfiber cloths for his birthday—because I smelled something unbelievably aromatic.

Salmon.

My discerning black nose quivered all over. It quivered in tiny little sections, thrumming with activity as I sniffed and sniffed. My nose is a radar that can pick up scents from inside grocery bags, under plastic wrap. . . . You cannot hide a scent from me. Stop trying.

And now this—salmon.

I did what I always did under the appropriate circumstances, which was to emit a clear, beautiful bark. *Rrruuufff.* None of that yapping and arfing that some dogs do. The key is to enunciate.

Just as in my most fervent dreams, I sat at the table with them, sitting tall in my chair, my poise evidence of my perfect poodle-ness.

"Can you believe how good she is?" Alison said.

Believe it, bud!

Alison gave me my *cookie*. Ted laughed. He slipped me some broccoli. He was not half bad, that Ted.

But no salmon. Not even a taste. These two had it in for me, I was starting to think.

It was after dinner that things really got bad. I had already listened to their boring talk—yap, yap, yap—and Alison's unnatural, high-pitched giggle while they spoke of things that had nothing to do with me or how good I was. They didn't even bother to throw me one of the squeaky toys Alison had packed. Instead, Ted locked my Alison in a hug, their faces smothered together for a long time. It was the most intense sniffing I had ever seen. Were they breathing? They were on the don't-jump-on-that couch, which didn't leave much room for me, although I did manage to snuggle in next to Alison's leg. At least I could be a tiny part of this unseemly event and make sure she was fine and didn't forget who I was.

"Dea, get down," said Ted.

Sir, I will not!

"It's okay, sweet girl. I'm right here. Come down to the floor," said Alison, patting the rug with her hand.

He invited me to dinner, and I didn't get any salmon, and now *this*.

After what seemed like infinity, we finally got ready to go home. Yay! But wait, what was this? Did Ted have to come, too?

"I'll walk you guys home," he said.

No need! No need!

Too late. I trudged along beside them, uncharacteristically glum. No one paid attention to me. Outside the lobby, Ted didn't seem to understand that his job was done here; he was free to leave. Don't let the door hit you, Ted. Instead, he mushed his face on Alison's again.

We finally escaped into the noisy elevator box and went upstairs. We were well rid of that Ted. It was just me and my Alison again. Together forever. We didn't need anyone else. We just needed Alison petting me, giving me belly rubs, scratching me in those special places, on and on without end.

But things were different after that dinner. Alison began to listen to all these new sounds on a machine in the living room. She even pulled me up onto my hind legs and held me in her arms as we moved together to some fast songs while she yelled nonsensical things like, "Disco!" The music made my ears pop up, and I didn't understand why Alison was laughing her fool head off.

"What a good dancer you are, Dea!" she exclaimed.

But of course.

Afterward, she would play some slower, softer music and move her body in ways that I feared would damage her hips and cause her to need the v-e-t.

She even began twirling, right there in the living room! I hid beneath a chair and watched from a safe distance, hoping she would stop.

I blamed Ted. Alison was never like this before he came along. And pretty soon, he was back again, taking her out to dinner. Had I not made myself clear that I did not like being left alone? I would never get used to it.

I fetched my green comfort blanket and whimpered. When that failed to bring Alison back in from the hallway, where she waited for the whirring elevator box to take her to the lobby, I tried something new and, if I dare say so myself, rather clever: I scratched at the big front door with my paws.

Nada.

Still, I was a hopeful poodle. One day I would discover the method that would keep Alison indoors with me, never to leave me again.

I grabbed my green blanket again with my choppers and huddled in a tiny ball of misery near the door. I would do this until she got home. If she ever got home.

I awoke from a lovely dream in which I was very nearly the victor over a *squirrel* that mocked me when the front door opened—and look what the human dragged in! It was Ted again.

As usual, he petted me along my back right away, no doubt thinking it would mollify me. Which it did. That Ted fellow was not so bad.

"Let's go to your room," he said to Alison, and I thought that was a marvelous idea. All three of us on the bed, cuddles, kisses, petting.

But no! Evil Ted had other plans!

Apparently, Alison was in on the horrible scheme because she distracted me with, "Dea, *cookie!*" Like a fool, I came running. And while I was busy with my *cookie*, the two of them went into the bedroom and a very bad thing happened—they shut the door on me!

Surely, it was a mistake. I scratched on the door to remind them to get their priorities in order.

"Dea, no. Stop," I heard Alison say, her voice muffled.

I continued to scrape the door, but to no avail. There were soft noises coming from inside our bedroom. I pricked my ears up and moved them around like antennae. Dogs have more than a dozen muscles in their ears, just another reason why we are so higher up the food chain than humans—whom we love dearly, but come on. Can they move each ear independently and in different directions? I don't think so.

I heard moving and rustling of sheets and strange sounds, like sighing and panting. What could they be doing?

Finally, and I mean after cobwebs had grown over everything, after seasons had changed, after the world had ceased spinning, the door opened, and Alison came out wearing what she usually only wears after a shower, a fluffy robe. She seemed relaxed and calm, almost like she was floating.

"Okay, Dea, you can come in now," she said.

I scooted myself onto the bed where Ted was still lying, and I pressed myself up against his large body. I liked when all parts of my body were touching another body. It made me feel safe. The horribleness of separation from Alison was over and would never, ever happen again.

But it continued to happen. All the time. Ted was always coming over, lulling me into a false sense of security with his deep back rubs. I gave him kisses of ecstasy. And how would these two traitors reward me? By locking me out of the bedroom until they finished moving the sheets around and smothering each other and panting. Only then would Alison emerge from our bedroom, always in the shower outfit.

At least they let me in after they finished their silly game, and I lay between them on the bed with every part of my body in contact with parts of theirs. Of course, I still had to endure their endless yapping.

"It's so easy being with you," said Alison with a dreamy sigh.

"That's ironic," said Ted, "because I've been told I can be selfish."

"No!"

"Yes, sad to say. Controlling, even."

Alison gasped. "You're anything but!" she said. "You're generous with your time, you're patient. It's been so long since ..." Her voice trailed off as if she were embarrassed.

"I know what you mean," said Ted, stroking her instead of me, until I whimpered for attention. "It's been a long time for me, too, having someone I can trust, someone I can relax with. Not to mention ..."

"Yes, not to mention."

They both laughed for no good reason I could think of. Were they happy to have found someone willing to rearrange the sheets? Once again, I would never understand humans.

"So, how did others find you controlling?" asked Alison.

"They said we only did the things I wanted to do. Like skiing or waterskiing."

"I love snow skiing," said Alison. "I've never tried the other."

"I'd love to take you some time."

Ted looked into Alison's eyes instead of mine. I wriggled a bit to remind him of his faux pas.

"I just want you to know what you're getting yourself into," said Ted. He took her hand and kissed it.

"I think it's amazing that you are so open and honest," said Alison. "We all have shortcomings, but it's rare to find someone willing to acknowledge them and work on them."

Alison was wrong there—I do not have any shortcomings. I was born a perfect poodle and will remain so for all my days.

"And just to let you know what you're getting into, too, I'm afraid of losing people," said Alison. "I have lost too many people in my life, including my older brother, who I adored. When my parents divorced, they split the kids between them—oh, it's too much to go into. What I mean is that to love someone means you have to be prepared to lose them, because they go away or die, and it makes me feel so unsafe. So unprotected."

"You're beautiful, you know," said Ted, smoothing aside a lock of Alison's thick, dark hair that had fallen across one eye, like a shadow.

"Am I?" she said with a little laugh. "Tell me more about that!"

They both laughed like hyenas. So tiresome, these people.

Eventually we all three drifted off to sleep, Alison clinging to Ted's strong, muscular body the way I like to cling to my green blanket.

Precious

"And the best thing about it—it was written by Burt Bacharach!" Alison was screaming for no apparent reason as she ran out of our bedroom.

"Oh no, anyone but Bacharach!" shouted Ted as he ran out behind her.

They raced around like wound-up puppies and laughed their fool heads off. Alison's face was leaking, but it was different from when she usually leaks. I saw she was just being silly, like when I suddenly roll over—but poodles are brilliant comedians with an excellent sense of timing, and these two had no sense of timing or delivery and apparently no sense at all. They just laughed and giggled and talked nonsense. Yap, yap, yap.

"Wait, I'll play it for you," said Alison, pausing to fiddle with the little metal-and-glass rectangle all humans are required to carry at all times and sometimes talk to. Humans are always talking to clumps of metal and plastic. "It's called 'Wives and Lovers.' When I was in first grade, I had such a crush on the singer, Jack Jones, I cannot even begin to tell you."

"I'm more of a rock 'n' roll type of guy," Ted protested, but Alison had found the song she wanted and turned the volume up.

Alison sang along, swaying to the tune with one hand across her belly and the other arm half raised, as if she had an invisible partner twirling her around the living room. "This singer's voice made me swoon," she added.

"Oh, this is the worst!" said Ted with an exaggerated groan. "It's like he sings don't let yourself go to pot or your man will cheat on you and it's your fault."

"I was six!" exclaimed Alison. "It's sexy and old school, and his voice is dreamy, and listen, this is my favorite part. He sings about, you know, getting in the mood."

She sang along and tried to get Ted to dance with her, which he did in a half-hearted, lumbering kind of way.

"Ugh, it's so schmaltzy," he said. They laughed and laughed, and Alison leaked and leaked.

She sat him in a chair and told him if he really cared about her, he would let her play the entire *Saturday Night Fever* album.

"You're torturing me!" said Ted.

"Humor me."

"Okay, but you can't tell anyone about this. Promise?"

He sat through it obediently, the way I am obedient when Alison says "heel" and "stay," but his hands stayed clenched the entire time.

"I feel like I've been through the wars," he said when the music finally came to an end. "Have I proven myself to you now? Please say yes."

"Just one Barry Manilow song?"

"Noooo!"

Ted made a fake screaming sound and suddenly bounded from the chair, making me jump. He ran after Alison and pretended to chase her. He laughed and she laughed, and she leaked, and suddenly, somehow, they ended up back inside our bedroom again with the door closed and with me stranded on the other side. I scrabbled at the door to show my displeasure, but there was more music playing on the other side, and eventually I plopped myself down with a dramatic sigh of the deepest despair.

They were going out more often. Without me. Sometimes they went to the theater, sometimes to a movie. Or they went to the Italian restaurant they liked, and Alison would tell me later about everything they ate, which mostly consisted of twisty long noodles with sauce and *cheese*. It made for a delicious bedtime story, although it would have been better if they took me along and let me sample some of those goodies.

On nights when they were not together, Ted always called promptly at 10:00 p.m., or at least that was how Alison described it. All I know is that every night at a certain time, instead of cuddling me—which is her life's work—Alison picked up the plastic box with the dangling cord and talked to it and called it "Ted" while she laughed and leaked.

"Oh, Dea, I have missed this so much," she said to me. "It's scary, though, telling another person everything."

But I knew this wasn't true. I knew she had not told Ted everything.

I knew what Ted did not know, that Alison went out pretty often to the v-e-t, the place with people in white lab coats, except it's for humans, and every time she goes to the v-e-t for humans, she gets very anxious beforehand and comes home in an even worse mood. It's something to do with a "diagnosis." It's something about a diagnosis that's the same as another one she once had, and whenever she tells me about it, her face leaks, but not in the happy way like when she tortures Ted with Barry Manilow. Sometimes she sits me on her lap and pets me a little too hard on my topknot while she talks to the plastic box with the cord and asks the plastic box for lab results.

"No, there has to be a mistake," she had told the box one time before Ted came into our lives. "Invasive ductal carcinoma, isn't that what I already had? I already went through all that. Look at the new tests and tell me what they say."

Whatever the box told her that time, she didn't like it, and she held me tighter and began leaking and leaking. I licked her face to try to stop the leaking, but it was beyond even my supreme poodle abilities.

Clearly, my Alison was in distress. I needed to find something I could do to make her happy again. Should I perform some antics? Usually, that worked, but it didn't this time. Maybe we would both have *cookies* together—she had her own type of *cookie*, but we liked to eat them at the same time—but she didn't seem interested in food.

She spent a long time talking to the plastic box after she asked it about lab results. She pretended the box was her friend Janie, and then she pretended it was Michael. She pretended it was lots of people, one after the other, and she told the box the same thing each time, that she was going to have surgery again, just like before, except this time it would be on the left side and without the support of her brother, David, who went over the Rainbow Bridge a few years before I brightened the world by being born into it. Just to set the record straight about geography, a subject I know plenty about because of all the walking in the park, David was not able to see Alba, my sister in heaven, because humans get a different bridge, one of their own. Alison and David's mom went over the people bridge a year after David. Alison seemed to think there was something wrong with the timing of that—that it was all wrong for a son to cross the Rainbow Bridge before a mother, but I really cannot be expected to keep track of everyone's schedule, so I tuned out that part.

"You're my only family now, Dea," said Alison. "My monkey girl. My angel girl."

Alison has a lot of different names for me, like "sweet girl" and "my love." Sometimes she puts them all into the same sentence and her voice goes very high up, I think to that point where only dogs can hear. Whenever Ted heard her do that, he made a face and said there's too much sugar, but he is not well attuned to musical sounds, as Alison had noted when he could not listen to Barry Manilow, and Alison's names for me are a kind of music. It was understandable why Ted could not get it.

Anyway, with the "diagnosis" that made Alison so leaky, she told the plastic box that when it came time for her second surgery, she would send me to babysit Sue for a day or two. Sue is someone who claims that animals are her business, that people pay her to look after them, but she is not very good at it, because sometimes I have to go and babysit her in her home and take her out for walks. The best part about her is that she always smelled of other dogs, and I could spend lots of time sniffing out just what she had been up to, and with whom, like the detective I am. When I took her for walks, sometimes another poodle twice my size came along, or a terrier type who pulled on the leash even more than I did, but I always managed to get it under control.

The problem with Sue was that she also had a cat. This showed a high degree of poor judgment on her part. The cat was so hairy it could barely see anything out of its malevolent eyes. Sue called the hairy white thing Precious, and I can tell you there was nothing precious about her. When Sue was there, Precious put on an act like she was a gentle, loving thing, but I could tell from her smell she was a killing machine dolled up as something innocent and trustworthy. Precious kept overriding my scent on Sue's legs. This horrible creature did not recognize that I was the alpha around here.

Also, Precious practiced witchcraft, which was not very nice of her. When Sue was not around, she sat way up high on the top of furniture that I wouldn't be able to jump on even if they allowed me, and fixed me with a Wiccan laser look, the evil eye. She sent me thought waves, but they made no sense. She sent me ESP messages that I was supposed to open a can of something for her, but I don't do things like that. Also, I don't know how.

Whenever I was about to curl up with my trusty green blanket, Precious would slink over and stare at me meaningfully. She'd put out a paw, and with her talons try to pull a corner of *my* blanket toward her. This was not acceptable. I would have to discuss this with Alison. Boundaries must be enforced.

But I didn't want to burden my Alison. I worried about her the whole time I was babysitting Sue. I worried about her second surgery and about how long she would take at the v-e-t. I took it out on my squeaky stuffed zebra until the stuffing started coming out.

After an eternity, times two—yes, it's my math abilities again—I was reunited with my Alison. I dashed inside the apartment like an Olympic sprinter, but she had a bandage over the left side of her chest, and she refused to pick me up! She wouldn't even throw my toys for me to fetch.

In the end, I resigned myself to leaning against her right side while she scratched me behind the ears and tenderly touched her left side.

All that had been a while ago, but Alison kept going for check-ups at the v-e-t.

"I'm going to have to tell Ted about this one of these days, sweet girl," she said. "He probably thinks it's just an ordinary scar. I'd tell him, but I just don't know how he'll take it."

She put it off and put it off. There was never a right time. There was always something new happening that was more important, like when Ted asked her to go away with him for a weekend. He said the leaves were turning and it was a glorious time to be away.

"But isn't it your weekend with Lisa?" she asked.

"I'll swap weekends with her mother," said Ted. "It's not a problem. We do it all the time."

"Sweet, darling girl," Alison said to me, "he's taking me hiking! I love hiking; it's my passion. I did it all the time in Italy."

Italy is a place where all people do all the time is sit around eating twisty noodles with *cheese*.

If Alison was going hiking with Ted for two days, it meant I would have to babysit Sue again. That woman needed a lot of looking after. She has been walked by many different kinds of dogs in the past, but it takes a poodle pro to make sure someone is good and walked. Alison said I need a job to feel fulfilled, and Sue was someone who needed a lot of work. She hardly did anything to my standards.

Alison packed my star-shaped squeaky toy, my red lobster, and of course my green blanket. Ted came over and rubbed my back and waited for us to get ready so he could tear my Alison away from me forever and a day.

Ted's metal-and-glass rectangle made a shrill sound. Not only are all humans required by law to carry one but they must keep it accessible so they can pull it out and stare at it or talk to it in the middle of dinner or while other people are trying to say something. They stare at it so much, perhaps it is a mirror into the soul?

Ted stared at his rectangle and also talked to it. He seemed angry at it, and I hoped that was not against the law. I don't like when there's trouble.

"Where am I? I'm about to go upstate," he said to the rectangle.

Then he continued talking to his rectangle, getting angrier and angrier.

"No, I told you I'm away this weekend. We swapped. Didn't you get my text?"

He kept yapping at the rectangle, but Alison sighed and slowly began unpacking my squeaky toys and blanket. There would be no hiking, no weekend upstate, no babysitting Sue.

All in all, a triumph!

I lay at their feet in the bed while they cuddled.

"You must know what you mean to me," said Ted, stroking her the way they were both supposed to be stroking me.

"What do I mean 'to you'?" she asked.

Ted just gave her a mysterious smile.

"I need to tell you something," she said.

"I'm listening."

"I've had breast cancer," said Alison. "Twice."

He looked like she had slapped him.

"I'm so sorry," he said. "Why didn't you tell me?"

"It's not easy to talk about," she said. "It's why I can't see you next Friday; I've got a procedure coming up."

"Do you need me to come with you?"

"Oh, thank you, but it's mostly routine. I'll be fine."

"I want to be there, if you want me," he said.

She did.

A Taste of Turkey

When the leaves had already turned and were falling and making crunching noises on the ground, Alison and I jumped into the back seat of a big green car with two strangers inside, a man and a woman who were driving us to Ted's brother's house in Scarsdale, out in the suburbs. Ted had already gone ahead with his daughter, Lisa, to help prepare for the holiday.

Let me explain. Thanksgiving is a holiday when there are fabulous scents in the air and family members come together to eat and quarrel and eat some more. Alison explained it all to me. She told me about all the side dishes, but I had to wait for her to get back to describing the *turkey* and the tender, succulent slices of meat. She talked about the real meaning of Thanksgiving, by which I think she meant the *turkey*. No wonder people got so worked up about this holiday and practically keel over with gratitude. Can't say I blame them.

Alison wouldn't let me hang my head out the open car window, which is every dog's birthright. But that was nothing compared to the annoyance that came next—we stopped along the way for the couple in the front seat to pick up their son and his dog.

"The dog's a little nervous," the driver said with a chuckle.

Well, he wasn't kidding! When the car stopped, a terrier type tore his way into the back seat with Alison and me, trying to take possession of the entire space. What an absolute pill already, and he wasn't even cheerful like I am. He refused to sniff me hello. What a diss. Then he wouldn't stop yelping. Please. The couple thought it was cute and kept trying to reach into the back seat to pet him and encourage some more of his bad behavior.

"Sit down, Sammy!" was all they said, and they laughed about it, but I did not like it and neither did my Alison, who kept telling me what a good dog I was but said nothing to Sammy, who was not a good dog.

I don't know why people assume every dog has to like every other dog. Are all humans besties with each other? Do they have to be?

Sammy was a drag. I'd never met such a glass-half-empty canine! I liked car rides now, especially being on Alison's lap, but this dog was a pain. First, the nonstop barking. Then the yelping. Then the crying. When the car jerked to a standstill in traffic, Sammy threw up. Come on, Sammy, gimme a break. He got it all over his human's pants, so we made a pit stop at a gas station so the couple's son could clean it up. I thought that once Sammy had gotten it out of his system, so to speak, he would stop being so annoying, but he yipped and yapped all the way to Scarsdale, which was a billion miles away.

When we arrived, my pedigree was evident when I waited to upchuck politely outside the car. Like a lady, okay?

Ted greeted us after our appalling car ride and gave me a back rub before he even spoke to Alison. Again, he has his priorities straight. Then he smashed his face on Alison's and held her tightly. We were all together in one big familial hug, Alison holding my leash in one hand and Ted's hand in the other. It was a lovely reunion.

"Come on, I'll show you around," said Ted.

There was a massive fenced-in backyard full of grass I could pad along on and tree trunks I could pee against. I call that a fully stocked yard.

There was also something strange—a huge hole in the ground covered by a protective plastic sheet. "It's still too cold to swim, but when it gets warmer, we all splash around," said Ted. My ears lit up. I am, after all, a water dog with a waterproof coat and webbed paws. A natural-born swimmer, if I do say so myself.

As a city poodle, this was the first time I had seen such splendid places to run! I had a full day's work ahead of me to explore all that grass, and I would have to be on my very best behavior if I hoped they would invite me back.

Ted's daughter, Lisa, finally emerged from the house. We had all met one time briefly when she came by her dad's to pick up some clothing, and I can tell you she took an instant liking to me. To Alison, maybe not so much, but I do know how to make a bang-up first impression with my melting dark-chocolate eyes and endearingly clownish ways.

"Happy Thanksgiving," Alison said as Lisa gave her a stiff hug hello. I jumped up on Lisa's leg to let her know she was welcome to pet me and lavish affection on me, which she did.

Inside the house, people were everywhere, and you know what that means—lots of new scents to check out and categorize and memorize. Lots of work for me to do. I hung back at first, a little uneasy with all these new people, staying close to Alison until the scents were just too pungent and interesting to ignore. They wafted inside my quivering black nostrils and drew me steadily toward the kitchen. I was helpless in their grasp, even though the kitchen lacked a wee-wee pad and a water bowl. You would think people could prepare better for their guests, but maybe these people had not had the proper training. I will not pass judgment on people with poor training as long as they have *turkey*, which turned out to smell like heaven on toast.

Alison said hello to Ted's brother, Eddie, who was wearing an apron but stopped stirring something with a ladle long enough to give her an unexpectedly hearty hug. I saw Alison starting to smile and could see her shoulders start to relax. I wouldn't have to worry about her all day and could turn my attentions to the *turkey*.

"Dea, you're so little!" squealed a woman, who interfered with my path toward the turkey. She was Eddie's wife, Shelly. "Everyone, look how tiny she is!"

I beg your pardon. There is nothing wrong with being a thirteen-and-a-half-pound poodle. I have a gigantic personality.

Alison picked me up and took me to the living room, my head still pathetically inclined toward the room with the *turkey*, and Ted introduced us around.

"And this is my Dea, which means goddess in Italian," Alison said, as she always did, thoroughly embarrassing me. I would blush if not for all my curly black hair.

They were all friends of Eddie and Shelly, and I must commend that couple's taste, because many of these humans had very fine petting techniques. They also gave pets to Alison, with lots of hugs. I hadn't seen her so relaxed in ages.

People emerged from the kitchen with platter after platter of food. There were scents in the air I had only dreamed about. There was also a gamey *turkey* smell that made me smack my lips. Not to mention gravy that had a rich, piquant aroma and stuffing and potatoes that made me drool. I would even take the vegetables, if offered. I had become accustomed to the broccoli that Ted had been sneaking to me whenever he cooked and Alison wasn't looking.

Alison's seat at the table was next to Ted's. I sat on her lap, trying my best to portray my good-poodle behavior and not swipe things off her plate with my paws.

"Dea, you're being such a good girl!" observed Alison correctly. "Here, taste this."

I believe I had waited all my life to hear those words! *T-U-R-K-E-Y*. Succulent. Juicy. The way I had always imagined it, ever since I first heard about *turkey* way back in the past, which was this morning. Thank you, mama!

"May I hold her?" That was the older lady sitting next to Alison. Like so many, she was finding me irresistible.

"Sure," said Alison. "But no people food, okay? She's already had a taste."

The woman was gentle, and I could feel her heartbeat quicken as she stroked my silky, well-brushed hair. She deserved kisses and I gave them in abundance. One landed in her ear, which made her laugh. Her daughter reached around to pet me, too.

"You and Ted make a great couple," she told Alison. "I want to take a photo!"

We huddled together, with me on Ted's lap, and the woman took picture after picture. I photograph well.

Alison seemed surprised that everyone was being so nice to her. It's because her brother went over the Rainbow Bridge, I think. She seems to think that once your family goes away, there's no more family, nothing to hold onto—but she's got me to hold onto and pet. Plus, my dog friends are out there walking so many people, you'd think Alison could find a new family so she wouldn't be sad.

But maybe she was sad even before losing her brother to the Rainbow Bridge, because she lost him twice—the first time was when her brother and sister went to live with their dad when Alison was six and she stayed with her mom. "Nothing ever felt safe again," she told me.

My Alison did not get all the petting she deserved when she was little. This is why I give her extra kisses all the time. I am a regular saliva factory.

We left the Thanksgiving house after everyone said, "Well, I'm stuffed." I saw we could not leave until every single person had said this. Perhaps it is another custom for humans on Thanksgiving? A kind of a blessing over the food? They seemed happy about being so stuffed, and also a little bashful.

After the last person—a cousin, I think—finally admitted to being stuffed, Alison took me outside for a pee in the grass, and then it was time for Ted to drive us back to the city. Everyone said what they were grateful for today, and I decided I was grateful I didn't have to travel home with that wimpy little terrier, Sammy.

"I've got a treat for you," said Ted, and when I heard *treat*, I thought he was talking to me. Instead, he handed Alison a little bag with the biggest *cookie* I had ever seen; it was half black and half white, which meant half of it looked just like me.

"My favorite in the world," said Alison. "You remembered! Of course, I'm too stuffed for it right now."

"It's for later, sweetie," said Ted. "You know, I wish I could stay over tonight, but . . ."

"Oh, it's fine, we just spent a wonderful day together," said Alison.

I wagged my puffball tail furiously. This meant I would have my Alison all to myself.

In front of our building, Ted got out with us, and I thought, oh no, he's coming up after all—but he gave me a soothing pet on my rump and he and Alison smashed their faces together one last time.

"Tomorrow night, okay?" said Ted in a husky voice, as if he had a cold. If he would take his face off of Alison's, maybe he could speak more clearly.

"Can't wait," said Alison in a choked whisper. Maybe she needed a drink of water to clear her throat?

They smushed their faces again, and then my hopes were dashed. Ted changed his mind and said he would come up after all. "I can't stay away," he whispered. Both of them had laryngitis by now. "I'll drop Lisa off at her mother's and come back."

When Ted returned, they went into our bedroom like usual, but they both said they were stuffed, the traditional Thanksgiving blessing, so they didn't smother each other the way they usually did. They left the door slightly ajar this time and just nuzzled each other on the bed and talked in their laryngitis voices.

"I haven't felt this way since . . . Lisa's mother," said Ted. Lisa's mother didn't have a name, or maybe he didn't know it, because he never said it.

"Me neither," croaked Alison with the laryngitis voice. "I also haven't felt like this in a long time."

Ted put his mouth on Alison's again and I think he was practicing for an exam in CPR and first aid as they continued to strangle each other. Their bodies were locked together so tightly I thought Alison might be stuck.

"What do you think this means?" asked Alison throatily.

"I don't know, but I'm happy."

"I have something to tell you," said Alison. "Shall I tell you?"

"Tell me."

Goodness, these people did not know how to make conversation with those laryngitis voices!

"I don't know how to say this, so I'll just say it," said Alison. "I think I'm falling in love with you."

Ted didn't say anything for a moment, and I pricked up my ears to hear if he was just speaking quietly, but he wasn't saying anything. Did it get colder in here all of a sudden?

"You know, I love you too," he finally said. "Hey, let's have that *cookie* now."

They unlocked their bodies and went to the wee-wee pad room, where Ted took out the big black-and-white *cookie* and divided it equally. They each got half-chocolate and half-vanilla icing. Alison then gave me my own *cookie*, and all three of us indulged in a kind of *cookie* bliss.

Between the *turkey* and the *cookie*, I thought the evening had gone spectacularly well.

The Snow Was Powder

If I had to rate Ted on a scale of what really matters in life, I'd say he was pretty up there. He knew just how to rub my rump with hardly any training. Although he was taking up more space than ever in our bedroom these days, it was very comfy and felt so safe and lovely when I managed to wedge myself in between their two bodies and lie there, nestled between my two safe harbors, making sure there were always several points of contact between my body and theirs. I could usually score a two-handed pet—Ted rubbing my rump and Alison scratching just behind an ear.

We were a real trio. Pure bliss.

The only worry I had was about how the two of them often fell into a coma. Sure, they still spent time sniffing and strangling each other, but for long stretches of time they would lie on the bed like zombies, watching moving pictures play on a big box at the foot of our bed. They went into these comas with their eyes still open, glued to the box, and forgot to pet me even when I wedged myself between them and bumped them with my snout as a reminder. I hoped Alison would make an appointment with the V-E-T soon. She needed professional help to learn how to stop falling into a coma so often.

Then, the pendulum of fate would swing the other way and Alison would spray that horrible smell on her neck and they would walk out for "a night on the town." Who needed that? A night on the don't-jump-on-that couch is all anyone really needs.

I did my best to stop her. I did the pleading look where my chocolate-brown eyes got big and melting and soulful. I did the little whimper, like I was too frail and helpless to manage a full sound. When those time-tested techniques failed to work, I went to level two: I groaned and beat on the door the moment they were on the other side of it.

When I could hear the big mechanical elevator box approaching, I had to pull out the big guns. It was time for level three. I moaned at the top of my lungs, making it as pitiful and desolate and woebegone as possible. Hey, I'm a drama queen. I've got this.

"I can't leave her like that," I could hear my Alison say on the other side of the door.

My heart lifted.

"She'll stop as soon as we leave," Ted responded.

My heart fell.

What a mean, horrible person. I never liked that Ted, despite the back rubs. Now he was showing his true colors.

The elevator box came and took them away, far away. Life could not get bleaker. I scrambled to find my green blanket and held it in my teeth, allowing its magic properties to slowly pacify me and help me get through this insufferable time until my Alison returned, if ever.

I fell into a deep sleep, where I saw—clear as day—a *squirrel* that obviously wanted me to chase him. I ran and ran, my ears twitching in excitement, my paws prancing in the air as I slept.

The *squirrel* climbed a tree. Once out of my reach, he stared down at me, triumphant. Mocking me. One day, I will get him. Oh, yes sir, I will get him.

Thanksgiving had been a lovely holiday, and the humans must have enjoyed it, too, because not too long afterward, they came up with another holiday, in December. Everyone got presents, but mine was the best—I got the wrapping paper once it came off the useless stuff people kept inside it. They would tear off the paper, and the paper was mine for tearing, shredding, and grr-ing at. Ted gave me some paper to chew, and it was still wrapping something, which turned out also to be for me: a red jacket with a hood. Alison seemed to like it, because it had been such an icy December and she was always putting little booties on me, but it was the crunchy, crackly paper covering the red coat that really floated my boat.

I also got an orange lion with a chewy mane. The lion made the perfect sound when I crunched on it—like a loud trombone!

"Ugh, I didn't realize it was so piercing," Alison said when I crunched and crunched.

I also got wonderfully crackly paper that had covered new booties so my pedicured paws wouldn't slip and freeze. Hey, just try to get these on me, lady. Hah! Good luck.

Ted opened his present and tossed away the paper—poor Ted does not have much in the IQ department, I fear—and instead paid attention to the soft gray pullover sweater inside it.

And Alison, who really should have known better, also threw aside the paper that covered a little box. Inside the box was a chain with a heart on it.

"Oh, I love it!" she said, and she put it around her neck and acted like it was better than a black-and-white *cookie*. "I'm never taking it off!"

At midnight, everyone gave everyone else kisses, including me.

"I'm not much of a holiday person, but you made this year the greatest I've had in years," said Ted. I wagged my tail to show my humble gratitude, but Alison seemed to think those remarks were meant for her, and they smashed their faces together and forgot all about little ol' me.

The next week, Ted pulled off a magic trick that was really quite impressive. I hadn't known he had it in him. He picked up Alison's plastic box with the cord and talked at it, just like Alison did, but then he pushed a button, and we could all hear the plastic box talk back to him! I have underestimated these humans.

"Hey, Jack. Just wanted to wish you a happy New Year," he said to the box.

"Same to you, buddy," said the box. "Do anything special?"

"I spent it with Alison."

"You still feeling unsure about her?"

Alison froze—I could sense her body stiffen—and Ted pushed the button again, and although he kept talking to the box, the box was silent in return. He yapped and yapped at the box, and paused, and then yapped some more.

"What was that all about?" Alison asked when Ted put the box away.

"That was Jack," he said. "Just firming up plans for skiing."

"He asked if you were still unsure about me."

"Sorry, didn't mean for you to hear that, but it's nothing," said Ted. "I haven't talked to him for a while. I was unsure when we first got together, but that's only natural. It took a while for us to be, you know . . ."

"I don't know. Tell me."

"Aw, Alison, you know how I feel about you."

"Do I?"

"C'mon, don't be that way."

He folded her into his arms. I tried to squeeze myself in there between their legs, but there wasn't room.

They smushed their faces together.

"I made plans with my pals a long time ago," said Ted. "Nothing to hide. Skiing in a couple of weeks and golf in Florida in April."

"Okay, but I don't want to be a part-time girlfriend. It reminds me of when I was a kid after the divorce, and I had to schedule time if I wanted to see my father and my sister and brother. I don't want to be an appointment that gets bumped from the calendar when it rains."

"It's not like that," said Ted. "It will never be like that."

"Will I meet your friends?"

"You'll meet all of them, I promise."

Some more smushing.

"Hey, I'd love to take you for a ski weekend," said Ted with his laryngitis voice, all clammy and deep. "Just you and me. Our own little winter wonderland."

"I haven't skied in ages, but I'd love that!" Alison burbled. When she was not in a coma with Ted, sometimes she got all congested like that.

I was very excited about the ski trip until I realized they hadn't invited me. Once again, I would have to babysit Sue.

Well, Sue needed a tremendous amount of my help this time because she also had a shih tzu puppy named Zennie at her place. This puppy was in no way qualified to babysit Sue. He needed constant attention and kept trying to nip my tail. I set him straight with a whack on his mouth. Hey, puppies need to learn boundaries, just like humans.

The puppy ran around and around until he just conked out on his yellow doughnut. That was cute, until he later tried to crawl into my blue doughnut with me and snuggle when I had just been *so close* to capturing the *squirrel* in my dream. I really would have had him this time, if not for that shih tzu.

Sue had forgotten her training since the last time I babysat her. The puppy and I frolicked with our squeaky toys, seeing who could pounce harder and make it squeak louder. That is a good game. But Sue didn't seem to know how to play. She invented her own game where she kept putting her hands over her ears, which did not seem like a fun game at all. She really was hopeless. That must be why so many dogs had to walk her each time, like a pack of ten with ten separate leashes all wound around her wrist. She could not be left alone for a moment, that one.

Also, I didn't want to bring up this sordid subject, but Precious the pernicious cat was there, too. Precious was always hatching evil plans. I could see her very few brain cells hard at work devising schemes to steal my green blanket or undermine my confidence in other ways. I was sitting there minding my business, chewing on my Nylabone, when Precious came over and swatted me—for no reason! Unbelievable.

I was so busy walking Sue and fending off the nipping puppy and avoiding the evil Wiccan ways of Precious that eternity passed quickly, and once again my Alison was home. She yapped away and told me about every second of her time without me.

"The snow was powder!" she exclaimed.

I wondered if the powder made her sneeze or left dust on her clothing, but she said it was a good thing, like out west.

"Oh, my sweet girl, I wish you could have seen it," she said.

She described it and described it until I didn't really want to hear about white powder ever again—not if I hadn't been there with her to experience it—but I let her go on because I was so happy that she was home and would never, ever leave me again.

"Ted booked me a private lesson," she said. "At first, I was wobbly, but after a few runs on the baby slope, I felt my ski legs return. The instructor was so patient. Then he took me on a ski lift a lot higher, and there was Ted, waiting for me with a grin."

The teacher told Ted that Alison was not half bad—which I think means that she was half good, which I can certainly vouch for—and Ted took her on an advanced blue run, much more difficult than she had ever tried.

"I felt terrified at first because I had never gone past the green runs. But it was more thrilling than I could have imagined," said Alison. "Exhilarating. The feeling of being in perfect harmony with the mountain and with nature. And, sweet girl, with Ted."

They went on higher and steeper and riskier runs. Alison said she felt like she was flying. "When you already feel safe, you believe you can accomplish anything," she said, although by now we were lying on our bed and she seemed to be talking to the ceiling, or to herself, and had forgotten all about me. "Ted couldn't believe it had been so long since I skied. Even after I fell on an icy patch, he helped me up and was so concerned. He insisted we ski back down to the lodge and have hot chocolate. But I did another run anyway, and on the lift back up, he pulled my ski mask away and kissed me."

He kept smushing his face on hers while her toes and fingers and face got numb from the cold. And then he whispered something in her ear, but she couldn't hear it over the whistling wind.

"What's that?" she yelled.

He said it again, louder.

"I love you," Ted shouted.

Alison told me his words set off a delicious feeling right through her body. She almost wanted to make him say it again, just for the rush, but there are laws for humans that you can't make other people say that to you too many times, or they change their minds about it and withdraw their love completely.

A Natural Swimmer

We began to see more of Lisa, Ted's daughter. I flapped my tail madly whenever I saw her and gave her the best kisses. She was really warming to me. Frankly, how could she not?

We did things with her sometimes on the weekends. Weekends are the times when humans are allowed to stop hunching their shoulders like the weight of the world is on them.

Lisa kept losing things in the park, and I'd have to bring them back to her. Sticks, toys, you name it; it's like she couldn't hold onto anything. I was very good about retrieving her items and returning them to her, but Alison never let me off the leash, so Lisa would have to run alongside me, and I am a terrific runner. Even Ted said so, although I think he said a "beautiful" runner. I can live with that.

My Alison is not a good runner. She says she runs all the time at the gym, but I never see her run in the park when I'm out walking her. I guess that's why Lisa never threw anything for Alison to run after; maybe Alison does not know how to fetch.

It was because of Lisa that I finally got off the leash. We took a car ride with her and Ted to Ted's brother's home in Scarsdale, a sacred house enshrined in memory where I once had *turkey*. That was many moons ago, many moons worth howling at, all the way back in November. The weather now was completely different, but I remembered it so well that I drooled just looking at the front door when we pulled up. Alison has gaps in her memory, like exactly when to feed me—which should be more often than she does—but my memory is infallible, at least when it comes to *turkey*.

Eddie and Shelly came out to greet us and petted *me* first before they petted Alison. Did I mention they have exquisite taste? I needed to pee, but I could see that petting me meant the world to them, so I toughed it out until they turned their backs. I am a rather private poodle.

"Does Dea want to run around?" asked Shelly.

Yes, Dea wants to run around!

"No," said Alison. "She's never been off the leash."

"The yard is completely closed in here," said Lisa. "Come see."

Bless that child.

"Let her run, sweetie," said Ted. "We'll sit outside with her and keep an eye out."

"But what if she jumps into the pool?" asked Alison. My Alison is such a worrywart. Did she mistake me for a silly Labrador who jumps into almost anything? Like most of my breed, I am quite circumspect. I do not jump into things before they are thoroughly vetted.

Well, I have to tell you, I ran and ran. I sniffed and dug. I leaped and nearly screamed in delight. I did not actually scream, because I've got breeding— that's what the breeder lady said—but my joy was off the charts. Grass, dirt, *squirrels*, smells. Ted's family didn't live in Scarsdale; they lived in Eden.

What was this? The flowers over here smelled a little like the horrible stuff Alison put on her neck whenever Ted came over, but lighter, less concentrated. What's that? A *squirrel* had dug here recently, maybe burying its nuts. I will have to check this out more thoroughly. But first . . . what is *that*? I darted here and there. Alison laughed so hard I thought she would need a v-e-t.

"She's a real athlete," I heard Alison say.

"Fast as a bullet," said Ted.

And then, a miracle beyond miracles. After lunch, Alison and Ted got into the hole in the ground with water and invited me in.

"She can swim, right?" asked Ted.

"Poodles are mighty swimmers," said Alison. "But she's never tried it before, so I don't know how much she'll like it at first."

Hmm, swimming. This is ringing a bell somewhere in the deep recesses of my excellent brain. Or maybe it's not in my brain, more like my bones. I just have this unshakable feeling that swimming is in my blood. That my mighty shoulder muscles can do something other than pulling on my leash.

Alison and Ted had changed into clothing that didn't cover very much of their bodies. Alison sat on the side of the pool with her legs in the blue water and me on her lap. Ted got inside the watery hole in the ground first and held his arms open. "Let her go. I'll catch her," he said.

"What if . . .?" said Alison, but she stopped herself short. Sometimes she would start saying "What if . . .," and Ted would interrupt her and say, "You worry too much," and she probably didn't want to start another round of *that*.

I plopped into the water and floated on top of it like I was levitating. I had magical powers. My stupendous shoulder muscles knew just what to do. I broke out into a perfect doggie paddle.

Lisa had gotten into the water, too, and squealed with delight. "Look at her go!" she yelled.

I got a lot of attention with my doggie paddle—much more than the humans did with their flailing attempts to swim—and I liked all the attention, so I kept paddling back and forth, back and forth. I could have done it forever, but eventually Alison hauled me out of the water.

Lisa laughed and screamed as I began to shake the liquid off my beautiful black curls. I started by shaking my head and long ears vigorously, like a fan turned on high, followed by my upper body and shoulders. Then, I jiggled my midsection like an exotic belly dancer. Finally, I shook my rear and my soggy tail. It all sent a delightful spray all over the backyard, even on Shelly, who had been trying to read a book in a lounge chair, but I'm sure she doubly appreciated the book once I had fully soaked it.

I was a bit tired, but oddly, Alison seemed to want to start a game with me of tug-of-war. She kept trying to throw a towel over my back and, okay, if that's the way she wanted it, fine. I grabbed one end of the towel in my teeth and pulled while making a fake *grr*.

"Let me dry you off," said Alison, but I knew she was trying to fake me out so she could win the tug-of-war, so I ignored her entreaties.

Like a real family, all of us ate outdoors together and soaked up the late afternoon sun. What a day. I didn't want them to forget what an exceptionally talented swimmer I was, so I pranced around the backyard with my topknot held high to remind them.

"You know, every year my friends and I go hiking in New Hampshire," said Ted once we were back home and he and Alison had finished panting in the bedroom and had opened the door for me to come back in. "You said you hiked a lot in Italy, so I was wondering . . ."

"Oh, yes!" said Alison. "Hiking is my favorite thing, hands down. Dea and I would love to come."

"You're bringing Dea? That might slow us down."

Hold it right there, buddy, it's you humans who slow *me* down.

"But she'd love to swim in the lake. I was hoping maybe you'd watch her for an hour so I could swim, too."

"Well, it's not until August, so there's plenty of time to work out the details," he said.

"August? That seems so far away," said Alison. "Maybe we could do something fun before that. You know, not just get in a rut of dinner and a movie once a week."

I wedged myself between them and did a thump-thump on their legs with my tail wags.

"What about waterskiing? The season is coming up, and I usually go out on the boat with my buds," he said. "But I know my friend Ronnie wants to meet you, so maybe we can do just the three of us. He's a hoot; you'll love him. Always joking around and pretending he'll drive the boat away while I'm skiing, like he forgot all about me. What a riot. Or maybe Jack will want to come. You said you liked him."

Actually, that's not what Alison said. After meeting Jack at a restaurant, Ted asked, "That Jack is something, right?" And Alison simply replied, "Right." Not exactly a ringing endorsement, but then Jack had been the one who had been inside the little plastic box and asked if Ted was still unsure about my Alison, which had made her a little distressed, so she wasn't in the mood to love him to pieces.

Alison told me she thought Jack was a sensitive man who had a bit too much on his plate. This is a people expression for other people who don't know how to bark "no" and wind up having too much to do, too many things to fetch, and too many obstacle courses to run. But in Jack's case, it really was about having too much on his plate, because he kept looking down at his bowl of pasta and never at Alison. If I had been there—instead of abandoned to a Bermuda Triangle of loneliness—I would have helped him by eating his curly noodles. "He seemed sad," Alison told me. "Ted and I spent the whole evening trying to lift his spirits."

"Yeah, I'll see if Jack can come, too," said Ted about the upcoming waterskiing trip. "Maybe he'll bring his wife. Wait till you see her—gorgeous. A ten ."

Alison blinked and didn't speak. Maybe the number ten and the blinking were some kind of code between them.

"Alison?" Ted prodded. "What do you think?"

"I think you shouldn't tell me what knockouts other women are," she said.

"Aw, you know I think you're beautiful, too. Anyway, you want to come? Dea would love it."

"I've never water-skied ."

"I'll teach you. It'll be fun! It's just like snow skiing, except it's not downhill and there's no snow and you need a lot of upper body strength. Don't worry, it won't be a problem."

The waterskiing trip happened on a weekend, which is the only time the law allows humans to have fun. The laws seem to be very strict about this. The rest of the week is for slogging around with their shoulders hunched in misery.

We drove to a lake in northern Westchester, about an hour from the city. Ted had bought me a pink life jacket, the color of which perfectly set off the silky blackness of my hair. I looked like a real seafarer. Alison had a life jacket, too, but it wasn't specially tailored for her, and it was a drab color. Didn't suit her at all.

Ted's friend Ronnie met us there and gave me a sturdy pet on my rear end. I gave him kisses in anticipation of my water adventure. I was kind of hoping Jack would come with the gorgeous, "ten" wife, because if his plate was still full, I was really going to help him out with that.

In my pink life jacket, I walked all around the dock with a confident step. It was a breezy, sunny day on the lake, and the sun felt glorious on my face. My ears blew backward in the wind. The water glittered. I hoped they would let me swim now that I had proven myself a champ in the sport.

I thought that just floating around on the water would have made for a perfectly fine day, but suddenly they revved up the engine and it was time for waterskiing. It was Ted's turn first while Ronnie steered the boat. Ted put extra-long planks on his feet and jumped overboard. I knew he could swim, because he had done it in the hole in the ground at his brother's house in Eden, but what he did next was simply astonishing, even better than the time he pressed the button on the plastic box and other people's voices came out.

He stood up on the water!

Ronnie made the boat go faster, shouting something about how he was going to leave Ted behind, and Ted laughed his fool head off about that. And then Ted started soaring along the top of the lake. He zigged and zagged, like I used to do when I first started taking Alison for her walks, until she made me stop that and walk straight, maybe because she has a poor sense of direction and my athletic derring-do confused her.

I hung my head over the side of the boat, staring in wonder at Ted as he walked on water with his big plank feet! He gave me a broad smile. When he was done, he collapsed into the water for a moment, which scared me. Maybe the spell had worn off and he was mortal again? But then he climbed back into the boat, laughing and shaking water off his body the way I shook off water after the hole in the ground.

"Okay, your turn," he said to Alison.

Alison put the huge planks on her feet, but she did it slowly and did not seem quite as enthusiastic. She waddled over to the rear of the boat.

"Just jump in," said Ted. "That's right, go ahead!"

"Al-i-son! Al-i-son!" chanted Ted and Ronnie. "Just jump in!"

They laughed their fool heads off, which apparently was the main thing they had in common, but it didn't make Alison feel any easier about getting in the water. They each thought the other one was so hysterically, mind-expandingly funny that they high-fived each other while Alison was hoping to get more specific instructions on how to do this water ski trick of walking on water.

"Does Ronnie have to drive the boat this fast?" Alison called over to them. "It's my first time, you know."

"Don't be silly," said Ted. "The boat needs to go a certain speed, like a rhythm, or you won't be able to rise out of the water."

I looked over the side of the boat and saw that my Alison was sitting on the water with those huge boards on her feet sticking up. The boat began to go faster as she held onto a rope. For a moment, she managed to get halfway up—success!—but then she disappeared into the lake amid a lot of bubbles and foamy water. The magical walking-on-water spell hadn't worked, and I couldn't see her anymore. I began to whine.

I don't think anyone witnessed this terrible thing except me. Ted was busy slathering on some foul-tasting sun lotion that wasn't worth licking. Then his hands were so oily he had trouble opening a big bottle of water. Understandably, he needed to hydrate, because no one had been thoughtful enough to provide anyone except me with a water bowl, and I was not in the mood for sharing—and why were these two humans not putting on diving equipment to go and search for my Alison?

After forever, my Alison reappeared from under the water, coughing and sputtering. She was still out of breath when she climbed aboard the boat.

"Wasn't that awesome?" said Ted.

She shook the water off herself the way I had at the hole in the ground.

"I'm never doing this again," she said.

Although Alison and I didn't go with Ted on his next few trips to water-ski and rub foul-tasting sun cream all over his body, she still spoke with excitement about the upcoming New Hampshire hiking trip.

"You're going to love it, monkey girl," she said to me. "It will be good to get away from the city."

But Ted never locked down the dates for the hike, and he was so busy with the waterskiing and his other friends that we saw a lot less of him. I liked having Alison to myself, but I noticed she didn't smile when she said his name anymore.

"He just takes me for granted," she told the plastic box, calling it Michael.

Then she argued with the plastic box. "That's not true," she told it. "I don't say it that often. Just now and then, and he rarely says it back anymore. I even had to ask him whether he still loves me. He said, 'You know how I feel about you,' which is the coward's way out, if you ask me."

After a brief pause, she was even angrier at the plastic box than before.

"Why not? Why shouldn't I ask? Tell me why it's so awful for a woman to say I love you and not a man. It doesn't seem fair. . . . I bought that book you recommended, the one about mutuality in bed, and he hasn't read it with me yet. He says things are fine the way they are, he's happy. But I just want to feel the intimacy we had before. . . . Yes, I told him all about page fifty-seven and all the other erogenous zones . . ."

Alison was not playing the special music and twirling around the living room anymore.

"I'm going to pick up the train tickets for New Hampshire later today," she told Ted over the breakfast she always made him.

"The dates aren't set on that yet, so no rush," he said.

"You're still not sure about bringing Dea? You'd only have to watch her for maybe an hour a day if I went for a swim in the lake. I really want her to come, and I know she would love the chance to swim again. Can't you just give me that? One hour a day?"

He lifted one shoulder instead of answering and pointed to his mouth to show he was chewing and completely unable to talk and answer her questions.

They went away for a hiking weekend in Connecticut, just the two of them, without me or his friends. I didn't know what kind of vacation you call that, one without me. Where was the fun in that?

I babysat Sue again—my goodness, that lady is hopeless, with a whole new pack of dogs having to walk her and Sue getting irritated whenever our leashes intertwined. And Precious the cat had gotten worse, if that can be believed. I was about to curl up in my blue doughnut with my green blanket and take a lovely snooze, when to my horror I found Precious already snuggled in there, making a disgusting rumbling sound deep in her chest! I tried to nose her aside, but she was like a big, hairy white ball of lead and wouldn't budge. I had to kind of figure out a way to wedge myself in there—in my own bed!—and try not to worry about all the bedraggled white fur she was going to leave behind all over my toys.

Needless to say, I didn't see Alison again for about a hundred years. Grueling. But not as grueling as her time away with Ted, apparently.

"It didn't go well, monkey," she said, burying her face in me. "We stopped to chat with a bunch of other hikers taking a water break, and when they mentioned they were hiking all the way to New Hampshire on the Appalachian Trail, Ted told them he was going there, too, at the end of the summer. He didn't say a word about us, baby girl. Not a word! And it sounded like he knew very well which dates he'd be there, even though he hasn't told us yet."

Ted and Alison always used to yap about uninteresting human things, like plays they wanted to see or countries they wanted to visit, but now all they seemed to yap about was New Hampshire.

"The thing is, I go with them every year, and with you there, it'll change the dynamic of the group," said Ted.

"That's what you said about your waterskiing group of buddies."

"Well, it's all true."

"So, you're disinviting both of us? Me and Dea? After keeping us hanging for months?"

"I don't think you'll have a good time. And I *want* you to have a good time, of course I do, but I don't think this trip is right for you."

Her face went stiff. I went over to her and nuzzled her leg. I knew that would help.

The next time Ted came over, the three of us lay in bed with the big box turned on with moving images and car crashes and booming music. Uh-oh, I knew what was coming next—yup, they both fell into that coma where they stared at the screen with their eyes open but nothing behind those eyes. I was really going to have to put my paw down about taking Alison to the v-e-t.

Finally, Ted spoke. Thank goodness the coma had not completely set in yet.

"Wow, she's sexy," he said.

"Who?' asked Alison.

"That girl on the TV," he said. Ted's eyes kind of popped out of their sockets for a moment with a *boing* sound, or maybe that was my imagination.

"Wasn't she in that other show?" he said. "You know the one I mean."

It was the first time I could recall that Alison wasn't interested in sharing a black-and-white *cookie* with him. When she got out of bed, she threw my green elephant toy like she was mad at it.

She took off the necklace Ted had given her, the one she had said she would never take off, and we never saw him again. Now that it was just me and Alison, like in the old days, I didn't even miss him.

The Men Online Who Are Too Hot to Wear Shirts

It was a blissful time. I like to refer to it as the Golden Age. "This is your place to sleep now," said Alison, patting the side of the bed where Ted used to sleep.

She didn't spray foul odors on her neck, and she didn't go out and leave me alone much at night. All those times I had beaten on the big door must have paid off. We snuggled together in bed, looking at the box with pictures, not falling into those comas I used to see Alison and Ted doing. We just watched with sleepy contentment.

One evening, she did something a little strange. She put me on her lap while she sat at her desk looking at pictures of men "online." There were a lot of men at this place "online." It was a special place where men put pictures of themselves looking sporty and sometimes forgetting to put a shirt on. It must have been a very warm temperature "online," because a lot of these men could not bother themselves to put on a shirt.

"Ooh, Dea, this one likes dogs!" she exclaimed a little too loudly into my delicate ears. "No, wait, he's looking for 'fun,' and I think that's a code word for no commitment."

It was actually very nice, our new routine of settling in at the desk chair for a spell each evening while we had story time, where Alison talked about the men "online," many of whom still sadly had no access to air conditioning and had to take their shirts off for their pictures. They posed in ways that looked very artistic and showed off their strong profiles or their favorite hobbies, like holding a tennis racquet.

"Here's another one who likes to walk on the beach in the rain," said Alison. "These guys must be drenched all the time. I just can't believe what they write about themselves."

When she found one who liked to sail, my ears perked up. I did miss my pink life jacket and the excitement of being a sea captain. But she passed over that one, and I began to doze as she rambled on about Rick, who found insects fascinating, and Dmitri, who didn't seem to do anything for a living but insisted he had what the ladies love. I wonder what that was.

"Dea, this guy looks interesting, an orthopedist," she said. "That's a bone doctor."

The bone v-e-t held her interest for quite a while, and she kept sending him messages, asking if he liked poodles—as if that was ever in doubt! She seemed to like his answers, but when she asked him what hospital he was affiliated with, he suddenly stopped responding. His words vanished from the screen.

"It's okay, monkey girl," said Alison. "Better to find out now."

The Golden Age continued, with Alison telling me the stories of the men trapped in the unbearable heat "online" while she rubbed my butt and I kissed her face all over, until one day when the unthinkable happened: The Golden Age ended abruptly, and we were back in the Stone Age, with Alison spraying foul-smelling liquid on her neck and going out the big door at night. She said she was on her way to meet an eye v-e-t, which to me was simply unacceptable. Even though I trotted out all my acting and dramatic skills to stop her, turning my chocolate-brown eyes into melting pools of abject need, nothing seemed to work. She fed me my dinner early, promising she was just going "for drinks" and would be back "soon," but I knew it was a lie and that she was abandoning me forever and a day.

I seized my green blanket and sulked right in front of the big door. I didn't get to hear about what happened with her that night until many centuries and ages and eons later, when she came home and I happily tumbled into her arms.

"His name was Jeff," she told me, as if I cared about the name of someone who had dared part me from my Alison for even a moment. He had a very slight build and wore sneakers and jeans, while Alison had worn a summery floral dress. She had purposely chosen a restaurant nearby, "In case I need to escape," she told me—although why she would agree to meet a kidnapper in the first place is beyond me. She had been to this restaurant recently on our shared birthday with her friend Nina, and the manager had offered her a free drink for the next time she stopped in. She was looking forward to another special occasion when she could have her birthday drink; meanwhile, she wanted to patronize the place as much as possible to give their business a boost.

"Let's sit in the bar area," Jeff suggested. He ordered a *cheese* plate and water. Alison thought that was odd, since they were meeting for drinks, but I always love having a nice bowl of water myself, and I wouldn't mind a nice *cheese* plate, too, so I didn't see anything wrong with it.

"I'll have a pinot noir, please," she told the waiter. When it came, she swallowed a large mouthful and had to remind herself to slow down or he would get the wrong idea.

"First meetings are so awkward, monkey," she said. Yes, mama, that is why you must sniff him all over and kiss his face a lot. I find that takes away a lot of the awkwardness.

"Do you have your own practice?" Alison asked the eye v-e-t.

"I started years ago grinding lenses for a big chain, but I'm finally on my own," said Jeff. "I notice you squinting. Maybe you need your prescription checked?"

"I'm not squinting," said Alison.

What Alison was doing, she told me, was furrowing her brow because she couldn't find any opening for an easy conversation, but she didn't want to insult the eye v-e-t, so she only admitted this to me. She tells me everything.

The waiter brought the *cheese* plate, and Jeff began nibbling on it, and no wonder, because he was quite skinny. It looked to Alison like he needed a good meal. She wondered whether he ate at all, so she turned the conversation to food, and whether he liked to eat out.

Now it was his turn to squint like something was wrong with his eyesight. "I never do takeout," he said in a voice that suggested he thought Alison had asked whether he murdered innocent children. "I don't like the oil restaurants use. And I only use a specific salt."

"Isn't all salt the same?" asked Alison.

He stared at her. He definitely needed new glasses.

"It is not," he said. "I prefer pink Himalayan sea salt."

"Oh," said Alison, searching for a way to connect. "I've seen that in the stores. It's very ... pink."

She took another sip of her wine.

"And you like only certain oils? I know olive oil is very healthy."

"I only use organic first-pressed," he said. "What about you?"

"Well, I don't always have the energy to cook, so I like to order in," she said. She tried to steal a glance at her watch under the table while pretending to scour her memory for what she liked to eat. "I'm a salmon girl," she said, after seeing that her watch must have broken because it had hardly advanced at all.

"I hope you don't mean farm-raised," said Jeff.

"No, certainly not," murmured Alison, although in reality she had no idea what the restaurants sent her.

"You should only eat wild," Jeff proclaimed.

"I couldn't agree more."

Thankfully, Jeff had finished his *cheese* plate. He would not perish from malnutrition after all.

The manager himself brought the check and left it by Jeff's side of the table. "Happy birthday again, Alison—your drink is on us, as promised!" he said merrily.

Alison thanked the manager, but it was Jeff who looked really ecstatic. Now he only had to pay for his *cheese* plate.

After Alison spilled out her tale of woe about the evening, I kissed her face, certain that this time she understood that all we needed was each other. I was sure it would be the end of this nonsense.

But it wasn't. A few nights later, I was horrified to see her going out the big door again. "Dea, eat your dinner. I'll be back in a few hours," she said.

I was totally unprepared for this rotten turn of events and immediately sought out my green blanket, my only source of security in this cruel, uncaring world. It was beneath a toy in my crate. I clenched it with my teeth as I cried myself to sleep. I dreamed I was chasing that *squirrel* again, my nemesis—you know very well which one I mean, the one that leads me on and makes me believe I can catch him and then mocks me from a high branch. This time, I really was about to get him. I was so close to triumph. I was living proof that poodles rule. But the whirring of the elevator box down the hallway and the jangle of Alison's key in the door woke me from my slumber.

She was back! She had remembered I existed after all! I put on a great show of welcome to remind her there was never any need to go out when she had a perfectly good puppy right there at home.

We cuddled and snuggled, and she told me all about her evening with someone named Kevin, who she thought was an imposter because he did not look a single bit like the photo he had posted in the hot zone they call "online." In the photo, Kevin had been playing baseball, flexing biceps bigger than the bat he was holding. In person, his shirtsleeves hung loose on his arms. "I know it's not nice to say, Dea, but I have more muscle tone than he does."

She had ordered her usual glass of pinot noir, realizing she really needed that splash of wine to help her get through those first dates with the men from that place "online" where everyone had extra muscle tone.

"You go ahead, I don't drink," said Kevin, but he seemed perfectly nice. They talked easily, and they both liked theater, movies, and books.

Kevin was an actor, and Alison was very excited to talk to him about his craft, because she had tried it herself.

"I even moved to Rome for three years and got a small part in a Stallone film that was shooting there. I had another role in an Italian film, but they cut my part because I didn't have the necessary work permit at the time. Actually, I did get the permit later, but it just wasn't in time for that one film. Don't you just hate when you lose your best work in the editing room?"

"I've never been in a movie," said Kevin.

"Oh," said Alison. "But doesn't that happen in TV, too?"

"Never been on TV."

She was getting confused and thought maybe having one pinot noir was too much for her. She'd have to have spritzers from now on if she wanted to stay sharp.

"So, you're . . . in theater?" she asked.

"Anyway, Stallone is great," said Kevin, oddly, because he never did say what kind of actor he was. "He da man!"

"Yes, he certainly is da man," said Alison. "But I wasn't in any scenes with him. I played one of the workers in the control room who starts to panic before the explosion blocks the Holland Tunnel."

"Cool," said Kevin. "Hey, show me your best control room panic face."

This was not hard for Alison to do. She allowed her emotions about trying to flee her date take over and indicate the panic she felt about wasting another night of her life with a man she would never see again. The waiter had only just arrived with their food, so there was plenty of time to go.

"Wait, waiter," said Kevin, frowning at his meal. "Does this have any gluten?"

The waiter gave a half shrug.

"No, no," said Kevin. "I have an intolerance. Can you make it without?"

The waiter whisked Kevin's plate away to the kitchen to have the chef redo his meal.

"Sorry," Kevin said to Alison. "Gluten makes me bloated and gassy. But you go ahead and eat. Enjoy!"

It was a good thing Alison wasn't still with the eye v-e-t, because her brow was deeply furrowed by this point and the guy would have insisted that she get new glasses.

"So," said Kevin while Alison took minuscule bites of her food. "Rome."

"Yes, Rome," she said. "I lived there for three years. I also did some dubbing work there, and a large part of my first book takes place while I lived there. It's a memoir: *A Place Called Grace*."

"Cool, I'd love to read it," said Kevin. After an awkward silence, he added: "And Stallone, he da man!"

"He certainly is."

By the time she finished her last bite, Kevin's gluten-free meal had arrived.

I felt her pain. I really did. That's why I had crunched my crinkly lion toy earlier in the evening, to make things magically go faster for her. When she had first come in the door, she grabbed me in her arms and held me just a little too tightly, a sure sign the evening hadn't gone well.

"Oh, monkey girl, it feels hopeless. No one is right for me," she said. "Or for us."

When these evenings didn't go well—and thankfully none of them did—she would crawl into her bed and hold me close. I snuggled closer so she wouldn't leak.

But my Alison didn't give up easily. "Dea, you know you are my number-one monkey girl, but wouldn't it be nice if we had someone worthwhile, maybe someone who had a place with some outdoor space where you could run around again? Someone who treated both of us well?" If she wanted my honest opinion, I'd say it was good that she realized I am her number-one monkey girl, because I didn't want to have to share her with anyone. But if I did have to share, even a little, I agreed it would be far better to find someone who had grass for me to run on and *turkey* in the kitchen.

But she did not listen to me. The next guy on her stupid dating list had neither grass in his garden nor *turkey* cooking in his kitchen. Alison thought he might be interesting because although he lived in New York, he was originally from Italy.

"Dea, look at his picture. He's cute, right? And he speaks Italian. I can practice with him. *Fantastico*! I'll bet he cooks a mean spaghetti."

What was a mean spaghetti? I'd tasted spaghetti, although I needed to work on my twirling technique. But that had been nice spaghetti, not the mean kind.

She wanted someone who treated us well, so I was sure she would give up on this Italian guy. At least he managed to wear a shirt in his photo, but his bio had said nothing about grass or *turkey*.

Well, I could not believe my nose, because the night she went out with the Italian chap, she squirted that awful stuff on her neck. Why did she keep doing that to me? I wondered what she did to torment her less-favored monkey girls.

"Dea, I'm having drinks and appetizers with Enrico, so I won't be home too late," said Alison. "Go eat your dinner, and I'll be home soon." Again, that stupid word "soon." It means nothing to me. But for the sake of diplomacy, I agreed to chow down before indulging in my whining and whimpering.

I only heard about her evening later, of course. Always the last to know. It appeared that Alison met Enrico at a crowded bar, and they were able to find a booth in the back where it was a little quieter so they could speak some Italian.

"I'll go get us some wine," he told her. "*Rosso o bianco?*"

"*Rosso.* A pinot noir for me," she said, pleased already with his gentlemanly ways.

He returned with their drinks and some *cheese* and crackers to nibble on, plus a vegetable dip. Alison only dated men who liked *cheese*; that much was clear. I thought that was appropriate. "Food is important to Italians," Alison told me.

Enrico worked as an IT professional at a large company and had been living in New York for about eight years. "I come from a town east of Rome in the Abruzzi region. Pescara. Do you know it?" he asked.

"I've heard of it," said Alison. "I've lived in New York nearly all my life, but I lived in Rome for three years."

"I hate Rome."

"Oh," said Alison, a little taken aback.

"Too chaotic."

"Sure, although to me it was rather exciting."

Alison thought his answer was a good one, though. Here was someone who wanted a calm life, not a lot of drama. Someone who wanted to curl up with her and a certain poodle we know.

I think it's time I explained what a "first date" is. After hearing Alison talk so many times about her first dates, I have become a bit of an expert on the subject. A first date is when a woman finds a man "online," where he may or may not be wearing a shirt, and meets him at a bar where he eats *cheese*. First, she makes sure he owns a shirt and knows how to put it on properly. Then, they make "small talk," which is just a lot of yapping about nothing.

Finally, they move on to the important stuff—they discuss each other's dating history. If they have too *much* history, they are no good for dating. They are all used up. If they have too *little* history, that's no good either. It means they are hopeless. It's okay if they're divorced, but if they're divorced more than once, it spells trouble. Alison is very into languages and word games—she does Wordle—and she likes to spell "trouble" and then say she wants nothing to do with it.

So far, Enrico did not spell trouble. He had been divorced, but only once. Alison, too, had been divorced once. The arithmetic was definitely working.

"I have a teenage daughter who lives with her mother," said Enrico. "I see her every other weekend, so it's not too bad."

After that, the first date usually moves into some new territory. The conversation turns to whether the two people share anything in common. I don't know why humans can't just figure this out the old-fashioned way, by giving each other a good sniff in the rear. It would save them a lot of time and yapping.

The funny thing was, Enrico did not yap very much. He neither sniffed Alison's rear nor yapped, so it became impossible to figure out what he liked in life.

"I love to travel," said Alison, thinking that Enrico could respond in kind—he either liked to travel or he didn't—but the guy just sipped his drink and smiled and said nothing.

"Um, do you like to travel too?" she prodded.

"I guess."

It wasn't too promising, but Enrico seemed to like her. He offered to buy them another round of drinks, so he must have been having a good time. Alison didn't usually have more than one glass of wine in an evening, but since Enrico thought it was worth spending time with her, she thought she would give it the old college try.

I suppose I should explain that, too. The old college try is to keep doing something that clearly is going to result in abject failure, but if you don't do it, other people will say you gave up too easily and they will make you feel bad. You do not want to be called a quitter. That is a very bad word, and you only say it to people you hate. If you do find you have to say it to someone, do not put it into a sentence. Just say the one word with great force: "Quitter!"

My Alison is not a quitter. She gives things the old college try. She agreed to another round of drinks with Enrico, and when he returned to the table with them, she said, "*Grazie*," and suggested they now speak a little Italian to each other.

Alison was glad she had given it the old college try. They had some conversation in Italian, where she asked him again if he liked to travel—but in Italian—and where he answered *penso un po'*. The evening was quite a success.

"I'm taking my daughter to Italy for a few weeks, but when I get back, we'll do this again," he said.

"That would be *fantastico*," said Alison.

Weeks passed. Alison pushed some buttons on the metal rectangle the law requires everyone to have, tapping out a message to Enrico. "*Ti sto pensando. Stai bene?*" She was thinking of him and asking if he was well.

Enrico wrote back two days later to say he'd decided to stay in Italy and didn't know when he would be back, if ever.

"Oh, Dea, look at me," said Alison. "I'm so undatable that men actually have to flee the country."

It turned out Enrico had spelled trouble after all.

Female Bonding

My advice to other poodles is this: Be careful what you wish for.

I had decided in my thoughtful, scientific way that Alison should no longer have first dates with men who resided in the warm climate of "online." I used good poodle reasoning, and I was successful. She stopped doing it. She was all mine.

Instead of paying even more attention to me, though, she began talking to the plastic box with the cord more often, calling it by various women's names. She seemed to think these imaginary people in the box were her friends and that she needed to bond with them more.

Bonding, by the way, is when you complain about things over and over to your friends, and they complain about the same things, too, and they reaffirm to each other that they are right and other people are wrong and that the world would be better if they ran it themselves. Then they eat chocolate, and then they start in on it all over again. Alison calls me a drama queen—and I do have a stellar vocal moaning technique—but maybe I got it from her, judging by the histrionics she went through during her bonding sessions with the plastic box with the cord.

While Alison bonded with the box, I sat on her lap with my snout on the armrest of her chair, hoping for a good pet.

"No, Janie, I am not even going to look online anymore," she said to the box. "I don't see the point. Everyone is weird or rude or fudging their age or can't eat gluten."

Janie is someone who saved Alison's bacon in Rome. That sounds very delicious. "I didn't know anyone when I first moved there, and Janie saved my bacon," Alison told me. I hope Janie will save some for me, too.

Alison and Janie auditioned together for acting jobs in Rome while I suppose they stored their bacon in a safe place. It was hard finding those jobs, so it was nicer to team up together and share information and laugh about it later if nothing came through. "Oh, we really laughed about it!" insisted Alison, although when she told me some of those stories, she sounded to me like she was about to start leaking—but hey, who am I, just a poodle who looks quite fetching against any fabric backdrop.

My Alison is full of surprises, and she managed to do the trick Ted must have taught her: she pressed a magic button on the plastic box, and suddenly we could both hear the voices of all the little people stuck inside it. Now it was Janie's turn to get stuck inside the box, with her voice coming out from inside it. Best of all, not having to hold the box in her hand meant Alison could give me a two-handed pet.

"No, Alison, you have not lost your feminine charm," said Janie's voice. I wondered if Janie was comfortable cramped up like that inside the box. I wondered if she ever had to stretch her legs like I do, one leg at a time, sometimes accompanied by a big yawn and some shaking of my lovely, feminine jowls. "I remember you having a new guy every week in Italy."

"I was younger. I was cuter. I had better underwear," said Alison.

"You're the same size you were then because of all that time at the gym," said Janie. "Get out the lingerie and wear it again. You'll feel good about yourself! Don't let a few men with poor manners tell you how to feel. Go out with your female friends. Go to plays and dinners. Take walks. Have an adventure."

"My last adventure was in Rome. I broke two bones in my back falling off a chair while I was looking in the mirror trying on a new dress," said Alison. "They practically had to airlift me home."

"Okay, maybe not such *adventurous* adventures, but try something out of the ordinary. Break the routine."

It was getting close to my dinner time, so when Alison went to have a chocolate before her next bonding call with the plastic box, I pounced on my loudest squeaky toy—the star-shaped one that Alison had given me as a tiny puppy—to announce with its shrillness that I thought it was high time the bonding sessions wrapped up for the night. I'm all for bonding, as long as it mostly involves me and Alison. How much more bonding does anyone need?

I do agree that friendship is important, which is why I make it a practice always to stop and sniff the rear end of any dog I encounter when I'm walking Alison. My favorite female friend is Lola, and we bond aplenty.

"That's short for Lola Rock 'n' Rolla because she likes to dance to music," said her human, Jessie, which reminded Alison to tell Jessie all about my full name and what it meant in Italian. These humans never get tired of explaining the names of their dogs.

Lola was a mix of breeds and had light brown, almost blonde, fur. Her eyes were friendly and warm and looked like she ringed them perfectly with jet-black eyeliner. She always kissed me on my snout when she saw me, and although Alison didn't also kiss Jessie on the snout, she did give her little hello hugs because she knew Jessie from the building.

Whenever Lola saw me from afar while I was walking Alison, she yanked Jessie toward me. And if Jessie was slow in that way that humans unfortunately can be, Lola would stomp on the pavement like a pony impatient to run around. I called it her pony dance.

When Lola and I finally came together, we gave each other kisses, our tails beating in tandem to the fastest drum, and we got our leashes tangled up together as a sign of true friendship.

The same thing happened whenever I joyfully ran into Iggy the border collie. Iggy liked to sniff me politely from nose to butt.

"Iggy, short for Saint Ignatius," said Delia, his person. "Saint Ignatius modernized the Roman Catholic Church, and Iggy has modernized my furniture by chewing on it—if you know what I mean!"

The two ladies laughed for no good reason.

All this is to say that I did understand the need to bond with one's friends, I really did, but when Alison bonded with her schoolgirl pal Nina, it was a big mistake. I could see right away that Nina spelled trouble. She was always pushing Alison to "get out more." Without me.

"We'll do dinner and a movie," said Nina's tiny voice from inside the box with the cord.

Nina proved to be a very bad influence. Alison started going out a lot to meet with her and do things at places that didn't allow dogs. They did a lot of cultural activities—and here I need to pause and explain that cultural activities are when you go to things you don't really understand but you pretend you do, and you have to wear your nicest clothes or they will kick you out, or at least talk about you behind your back.

Nina kept coming up with useless new things to do that would take my Alison away from me.

"We should go to a singles mixer," said Nina's tiny voice inside the box with the cord.

"Why would we do *that*?" asked Alison.

"Come on, we'll meet new people. It's different from online dating, where it's easy for people to lie about themselves and you don't really know what they look like."

"I've given up on guys," said my Alison, the drama queen. "I've decided to become a nun. Or live in a hole."

"You won't be happy in a hole. You can't get dinner delivered in a hole. I say we give this a shot."

Alison got all dolled up for her singles party, which I found rather offensive. We are a double, me and Alison. I don't see why she should be checking out any singles action.

"I'll be back soon, monkey girl," she said. Although she gave me a *cookie*, she used that awful untrue word again, "soon," which means "never."

When she closed the big door, I moaned and whimpered until I heard the clanky elevator machine in the hallway take her away. It was eons later when she returned and told me all about her evening. She had finally learned her lesson that the only singles places she should be is at home with me, her double in life.

Alison got to the place before Nina and thought she had made a mistake and arrived way too early, or maybe it was the wrong night. There were multiple white couches with fluffy pillows, all set up for intimate conversations, but those conversations would have to be among females only, since by Alison's count there were about twenty women and only two men. The women all wore tight clothing that showed off the number of hours they had spent at the gym—Alison wore her go-to black slacks and a snug-fitting red top—while the two men wore any old thing from a pile of clothes they probably had on a chair somewhere.

A toned woman in a slim gold dress sat down next to Alison and said she was new to this and didn't know what to expect.

"I've never tried this myself," admitted Alison. "I don't have high hopes."

"I suppose it's hit or miss," said the lady.

"Right now, it feels like miss," said Alison. "There are only two men here. One of them is on crutches. Not that there's anything wrong with that. It probably gives him really good upper-body strength."

"Look, the guy on crutches is coming our way!" said the woman in gold, getting all excited and flattered. "Out of all the women, he's chosen us!"

She sat up straighter, with better posture, as the man hobbled over and sank down into a nearby chair. He sat there without saying a single word to Alison or the lady in gold or even looking their way. All he wanted was the chair.

"Are we that unappealing?" whispered the woman in gold.

"Apparently," said Alison.

Nina finally arrived and apologized for being late, but after surveying the room, she apologized for suggesting the outing at all. She was also sorry she had made an effort to look pretty and had even paid to get a blow-out at the salon. Nina was sorry for a whole lot of things all evening long.

"I feel like I'm back at Dalton," Alison said, remembering the high school dances that were so fraught with anxiety and dashed hopes.

Another woman gravitated to their all-estrogen group. She had dressed nicely in a summertime short black skirt. Her toes were pedicured and polished, but she looked despondent and reached for a solitary peanut from a plastic cup of them. The four women introduced themselves to each other and began the female bonding routine, where everyone echoed everyone else's complaints and all agreed the world would be better if they ran it.

"This is absurd," said Alison. "I'm going to talk to the other guy, the one without the crutches. Then, at least I can say I've given it the old college try."

"Go get 'em, tiger," said Nina. "We expect a full report!"

Alison approached the second man gingerly, but he must have been so astonished that someone actually wanted to talk to him, he spilled half his drink down his front.

"No worries, no worries, comes right out with club soda," he said in a rush. "Don't go anywhere." He raced toward the men's room.

Alison waited for him to reappear. He didn't. Maybe he was embarrassed about the wine stain. Maybe he had moved to Italy like Enrico and was never coming back.

"Well?" said Nina when Alison returned to the couch with the estrogen mob.

"I did a magic trick," said Alison. "I made him vanish."

The women laughed and bonded and occasionally gnawed on a peanut or a cubed piece of yellow *cheese* with a frilled toothpick stuck in it.

"You know what? The evening is not lost," said Alison. "I just realized that if we leave now, I can be home in time for the ten o'clock news."

The women laughed and made other jokes very similar to that one, about which TV show they would be in time to watch, and wound up having a pretty swell night in spite of it all. They exchanged numbers and called it a night.

Alison's key in the lock interrupted my dream of chasing the evil *squirrel*. Still groggy, I managed to stand on my two hind legs and give her hugs and kisses.

"Dea, I had an interesting time and a lot of laughs, but no food," she said. "Shall we have a *cookie*?"

Cookies are the key to life sometimes.

The Men Who Are
Still Too Warm
to Wear Shirts

M y Alison forgot her training. She went back to looking at the men who hung out, some of them shirtless, at that place online. I sat on her lap with my eyes closed and yawned as she read descriptions to me and pressed keys.

"You can do this. You can do this," she said out loud, talking to herself as she put on nice clothing and drew designs on her face with makeup for a night out. "Who needs Ted anyway?"

She drew a bow on her lips with a red crayon.

"I'll wear the sexy red top he always loved. That'll show him!"

I now knew that any time she fed me my dinner early, which normally I would have thought was a good thing, meant the tragedy of her going out the big door and leaving me forever.

A light-year is a measure of distance, not time. A lot of folks get that wrong. But it sounds like a long time, so I would say Alison did not get back that night until a light-year later. That's when I found out all about Dennis.

She met Dennis at the Italian restaurant where she used to go all the time with Ted. Everything about the restaurant reminded her of Ted, from the murals on the wall to the menu items she used to order with Ted. Suggesting to Dennis that they meet there had been a big mistake.

And it was a really big mistake because Dennis was really big. "Dea, sweet girl, he must have been seven feet tall!" said Alison. "When we were seated at the table, his legs kept bumping mine."

Every time they bumped legs, Dennis would say, "Sorry," and Alison would say, "No problem," but it *was* a problem, because she was uncomfortable trying to keep her own long legs tucked away under her chair.

"I saw you said on your profile you like art," said Alison. "I majored in art history in college. I love the Impressionists."

"Yeah, I go to a museum every once in a while," he said. "For about an hour."

"An hour?"

"My legs get tired."

Alison took a sip of wine to hide her confusion. She would have thought having such long legs would make him strong.

"Sorry," he said because he had bumped her under the table again.

"No problem."

She suggested the new Dutch Golden Age exhibit at the Met, since at least they had an interest in art in common.

"For an hour, sure," he said without much enthusiasm.

After two hours with Dennis, Alison was starting to flag. "Well, this has been fun," she lied while signaling the waiter for the check.

"First, I'd like a coffee and an apple tart," said Dennis. "Anything for you?"

Alison had to endure Dennis's apple tart as time slowed to a crawl. The waiter plopped down the check smack in the middle of the table, but Dennis continued working on his dessert like he was at an archeological dig. He stared at the check while he sipped his coffee.

"Who's paying?" he finally asked.

"Well, you did ask me to dinner," said Alison.

"I guess I'll do it this one time, but I expect the women I date to pay for themselves," he said. He put down his fork and dabbed his lips with a napkin.

When Alison got home, she was totally in need of a walk. "Dea, I think it's just going to be you and me from now on," she said as we walked around the block.

I couldn't agree more. We enjoyed a blissful night's sleep, just me and my Alison.

But in no time, she was at it again. She found a tenured sociology professor who had just moved back to New York after living abroad. He wore a shirt in his "online" photo, so at least he wasn't overheated. "If he's tenured he has to be on the level, right?" she said, more to herself than to me. "And with my master's in social work, we should have a lot to talk about."

I doubted it.

What Alison needed was an intervention. All the voices on her plastic box with the cord needed to intervene and get Alison some help for her unhealthy compulsion to bring a man into our life to anchor it, when all she really needed was me.

She fed me my dinner a little early, which spelled trouble. She walked out the big door, and I descended into an indescribable darkness until she finally returned and told me about her evening.

The professor's name was Matthew—he had already told Alison he didn't like "Matt"—and he was already having a gin and tonic at the bar when Alison arrived. She had chosen a different Italian restaurant, which was a good idea because I sniffed sadness whenever she went to the one where she used to go to with Ted.

They moved over to a table in the bar area. Matthew quickly finished his drink in a big guzzle, and when Alison ordered her usual pinot noir, he suggested they share a bottle.

"A glass is fine," she said.

At first, it seemed to go well. They spoke about the shared experience of living abroad. Then they got to the portion of the first date where it was time to talk about divorces.

"I had an affair with one of my grad students," he said. "Well, you know how it goes."

"No, I don't."

He proceeded to explain to her how it goes, something about cheating on his wife with a hot, young grad student and moving to another country with the girl.

"She said she wanted to travel with me all over the world," he said. "Frankly, I wanted to marry her, but she ended up returning to the States to see her family all the time."

"She must have really missed them, being so far away," said Alison, trying to put herself in the shoes of a hot, young graduate student who ran off with her married professor.

"She started drinking heavily," he said. "Waiter, another glass of wine here. Anything for you?"

"I'm good."

The story about hooking up with a grad student, even though Matthew seemed to believe it was as old as time itself, certainly took a long time to tell.

"And then, can you believe it? She wanted to get a dog! A puppy, of all things," he said. "Care for dessert?"

When the check came, Matthew picked it up and paid the waiter without hesitation. At least he was not a dog-hating cheapskate. Just a dog hater.

"I'd love to see you again!" said Mister I'm So Awful and I Hate Puppies before he went home to his nightly routine of having a brandy before tucking into bed, which did not come as a surprise to Alison, since Matthew had been drinking nonstop all evening.

"I have a nightly routine, too," she said. "I cuddle in bed with my puppy."

But my Alison is not a quitter! She always gives it the old college try! Soon after her evening with the heavy-drinking, cradle-robbing puppy hater, she received a text from a lawyer bloke. I say bloke, because his text came in while we were in the middle of watching a Travel Channel show about England, and I was trying to increase my vocabulary. Alison had cut me to the quick when she mentioned that border collies knew the names of all their toys and could also herd sheep. I wanted to try my paw at herding sheep the next time the occasion presented itself; meanwhile, I would just keep working on learning things like the many ways to describe the marvelous sounds my toys make: "annoying," "ear-splitting," "like a hammer drill." I can also roll over if Alison twirls a single finger, so never forget I have my own set of amazing qualities.

Walking Alison

Darren the lawyer bloke wore a shirt in his photo, even though he came from that hellish inferno of "online." He looked healthy and vigorous, even though he was not flexing his muscles in the photo like so many of the men in that world did. He lived near us and suggested meeting at the Trattoria Roma—but that is the restaurant with the murals Ted used to look at and the menu Ted used to order from. When Alison saw things on the menu that she used to eat when they were together—like "mozzarella di bufala" or "side salad," you see my expanding vocabulary?—she tended to look doleful. A carafe of still water could set off my Alison. She is sensitive like a chihuahua.

"Dea, I think I *will* meet him there," she said. "The memory of Ted needn't spoil everything I do."

But this is madness, mama! Please stop this insanity.

I shook out my body so hard I nearly lost my footing. With my scientific-method way of reasoning, I could see how it might play out: She would go to the Ted restaurant and the new guy would order the chicken parm, but my Alison would not leak and I'd be so proud. I could only hope she would still order the salmon so at least I could blissfully sniff her later.

Despite my entreaties, she gave me a *cookie* to munch on and went out the big door. The *cookie* helped for as long as it took to swallow it. I grabbed my green blanket and dragged it right in front of the door where her scent still lingered. My yearning for her return knocked me out and I fell into a deep sleep, where I chased that infernal *squirrel* this way and that, zig and zag. He was always just out of my mighty grasp.

Later, I heard all about the evening with Darren the lawyer bloke. He did not look anything like his vigorous photo. A scraggly, fragile-looking older man who could barely stand upright got up slowly and carefully from his barstool and, using a cane to lean on, came over to greet Alison. I agreed that sniffing each other's rear ends might not have been the right thing to do under the circumstances. He might have lost his balance.

"Sweet girl, I don't care if someone has infirmities," Alison told me. "And he could be the best lawyer in the world; it doesn't matter. What matters to me is that he lied. Maybe I'm the last person on the planet who doesn't use a filter on my photos, but I just want to know what to expect before I meet someone. I was expecting someone totally different."

101

The lawyer bloke had made a reservation for a table, which normally would have thrilled my Alison, but in this case, a quick drink at the bar would have been just fine. Then she could have helped him outside to his taxi and she could have come right home to *me*.

Instead, they walked slowly to their table, with Alison eager for her solitary glass of pinot noir.

"A vodka, straight," he told the waiter after they sat down.

"Pinot noir for me," said Alison.

She could hear the bloke's cane slide off the back of his chair and rattle onto the floor.

"Maybe we should order now, too," said Alison, hoping not to prolong the evening beyond the bloke's bedtime. "I'll have the salmon."

"Just a salad for me," said the lawyer bloke.

"That's it? Not hungry?"

"You know, my ex-wife loved salad."

"Oh," said Alison, confused. "And that's why you eat salad?"

"Yes. She helped care for me through two bouts of cancer. I owe her a lot."

"Sorry," said Alison. "I mean, sorry you got divorced and sorry you've had cancer twice. So have I."

"She still lives near me and comes over all the time. When I was in the hospital, she was there every day."

"Well, I hope you're okay now," said Alison, wondering why he hadn't asked about how she was doing after her own bouts with cancer.

"I'm in remission, but my ex-wife always makes sure I'm okay, and my ex-girlfriend calls all the time to see how I'm doing."

"Sounds like you do very nicely with relationships that have ended."

Darren chuckled. "You're funny," he said. "Has anyone ever told you you're funny?"

Alison wasn't really in a fun mood. He kept talking about his cancer, his hospitalizations, his career, and his exes. He didn't ask about her at all.

"I'm sorry for all your problems, but this is not a conversation," she said, as kindly as she could. "It's a soliloquy."

Darren the lawyer bloke didn't find her so funny anymore. He propped himself up with his cane and pushed away from the table.

"What are you doing?" asked Alison.

"I'm leaving."

This had never happened to Alison before, but the man actually walked away and out of the restaurant and never returned. The maître d' felt so bad for her, he came over and sat with her while she finished her salmon so she wouldn't be alone.

"This never happens to me," said Alison. "Never, ever."

"At least he paid before he left," the maître d' consoled her. He was a handsome Italian man who Alison would have been happy to date if he were not young enough to be her son.

"*Grazie* for keeping me company. *Molto gentile*," she said.

She sprinted back to the safety of home. Ta-da! I could smell yummy salmon on her breath. I also sniffed a sadness, maybe even a kind of fear.

"It's just not safe out there," she said, wrapping her arms around herself for a moment. When we cuddled together on the bed, I gave her all the necessary kisses.

"Dea, the universe is trying to tell me something," she said. "It's trying to tell me that no one will ever give me that feeling I had before my parents divorced and my family was split up. I will never be safe and whole."

No, mama, the universe is trying to tell you to rub my belly and all will be well.

There was a special sound associated with the texts that came onto Alison's little metal rectangle when the dating company had someone new to suggest that Alison date. The ding came in, and Alison looked at the little metal rectangle.

"I wonder if it's that jerk apologizing for walking out on me," she said. "No, they're saying someone new matches my criteria for true love."

She touched a few buttons and swiped on the glass. The world of "online" presented her with her newest, most perfect match.

They sent her Ted.

The Break

"Dea, we deserve a break!" said Alison.

Vocabulary alert: A break is when you take a time-out before you explode, which is a condition that afflicts a lot of humans because they are only legally allowed to relax on weekends and because they don't know how to let off steam by rolling in the grass. If they rolled in the grass more often, they would not feel they were about to explode, and they would not need a break.

"You and me, let's go on a short vacation, just the two of us," she said.

She had me at "you and I." But I hoped she didn't forget to pack my star-shaped squeaky toy and my *cookies*.

I took her out for her morning walk before we left for our explosion-preventing break. I saw a handsome brown-and-white cocker spaniel, whose human called him Chuckles. "What a cute name," said Alison.

"Yes, he's named after Chuckles the Clown. Because I love that old Mary Tyler Moore episode, and because he's such a clown!"

Chuckles was so new to me that it required copious sniffing of anal glands. Alison waited patiently while I ascertained that this was a dog I wanted to sniff again in the future.

We took a car service to a hotel in Connecticut. As soon as we arrived, I blessed the reception area by upchucking. Alison looked around, pretending it wasn't mine and that another dog must have done it. I really think she gave up on an acting career too early; she still had the stuff.

They gave us a large room with a rug that felt smooth beneath my paws. The big bed was nice and springy. There was a big box with moving pictures on it, just like the one at the foot of our bed at home. I guess these humans cannot live without a picture box at the foot of their beds in case they needed to go into a coma. All the homes I've seen so far have a big don't-jump-on-that couch, a little room full of clothing, and a picture box at the foot of the bed. This room also had an outdoor place to sit with a view of boats bobbing on the water.

Alison was lively and had a spring in her step. I suggested I take her for a walk in this new place, and when she saw my prancing and heard my gentle whines and humble urging, she agreed.

In the lobby—by the way, a lobby is a place with shiny floors where you keep slipping—a hotel worker came over and said, "What a beautiful dog! She's the Elizabeth Taylor of black poodles."

The hotel worker was mistaken. Elizabeth Taylor, whoever she may be, is the Dea of humans.

"Dea, isn't that nice? Go give her a kiss," said Alison. I dutifully kissed the hotel worker, but secretly wished I were back at home sniffing the rear of Chuckles, that interesting new cocker spaniel. I would be the judge of whether he was appropriately clownish or not, based on my acute sense of smell.

I took my Alison for a walk around a large body of water near the hotel. "This is the Long Island Sound, sweet girl," said Alison. "It leads into the ocean."

The water glistened and sparkled, with small wavy ripples on top. There were delightful new scents, too, including a robust salty aroma and a far-off storm approaching that I could smell but none of the humans seemed to notice. There was a deep, delightfully fishy odor, too, all the way along the water. I was truly in heaven.

We found grassy patches where I could do my business and other places near the water with stretchy chairs where we could spend our time inhaling fishy smells. Salt and fish, fish and salt. The air was an aroma palace.

Later, after I had room service—Alison fed me my dinner in our room, and she called it room service—we walked along a street and sat at an outdoor table, where Alison ate something fishy. I didn't want to encourage her, but she could certainly find a man if she just breathed that fishy smell on him a lot. He would never leave her.

She offered me a piece of bread from her plate.

"That's the best-behaved dog I've ever seen," said the waiter.

"Yes, she's the best girl," said Alison, and from that I knew I would get two *cookies* before bed.

Back when Ted used to stay with us overnight, Alison began sleeping with earplugs because Ted, who was so full of magic tricks, made a sound at night through his mouth and nose that was the exact imitation of an airplane taking off, over and over. It was quite a trick. Now the earplugs were a habit with her, and she had just put them in when she took them out and said, "Oh no, this will not do." It was because two people just outside our room were yelling. Even I felt some alarm and began barking in a protective way.

The man and woman outside continued to yap quite loudly until Alison put on her robe, the one she wears after a shower, and opened our door a crack.

"Could you please keep it down," she said. "You're making my dog bark and that will wake up even more guests."

The man outside repeated what she said in a nasty voice, imitating her. He reminded me of Boris, the white German shepherd who always wears a muzzle in the park when I walk Alison but who manages to growl at everyone and at everything. Boris is always so unpleasant, I feel no need to sniff him whatsoever. Plus, I never have the time because my Alison briskly turns us around to walk in the other direction.

Our door was still open a crack, and you don't have to tell me twice. It meant I was supposed to scoot right out and make a run for it. Which I did.

"*Dea!*" Alison screamed.

"Oh, *now* who's making all the noise?" taunted the German shepherd man.

Alison ran after me and tackled me in the hallway, which was a lovely game I wanted very much to repeat at the earliest opportunity.

The German shepherd man and his lady friend continued yapping at high decibels even when we were back in our room. Alison picked up a plastic box with a curly cord, very similar to what we had at home, and spoke to it, complaining about the German shepherd man and how we couldn't get a wink of sleep. This plastic box had special powers of its own, because right away a large person with big feet and hands that had a smoky odor came to our room.

"They just went inside, but they said nasty things to me, and I think they're drunk," Alison explained. "Can you ask the man to keep it down? Or even better, move him to another room?"

"He's a bigwig here, Miss," said the man with the smoke-smelly hands.

By listening to the conversation, I now knew a new word: bigwig. This was someone who stays all day on a yacht but sleeps in a hotel at night. A bigwig was someone whose room you can't change.

"Can't you just send him back to sleep on his yacht?" Alison pleaded.

The hotel man explained that bigwigs are people who can sleep wherever they damn please.

All night, the bigwig made noise, and because bigwigs by law cannot be relocated, Alison and I did not sleep well that night.

In the morning, right after I slid and slipped on the lobby floor and took Alison for her first walk of the day, we went back to the lobby and sank into one of the big cushiony couches. A woman with blonde hair and a sweet smile asked if she could sit with us a moment. I jumped onto her lap, and she scratched me behind my ears.

"Her name is Dea, which means goddess in Italian," said Alison, starting her familiar litany.

"Oh, you are such a goddess!" said the lady, which was true. "You are truly such a good goddess!"

"Her full name is Dea Della Vita. The goddess of life."

"I'm Steffi," said the woman. "I don't know what it means in Italian, but I'm the manager of the hotel and I wanted to apologize to you in person for what I hear was a difficult night."

Steffi seemed very nice, and I was enjoying the attention, although I smelled something on her that did not please me. I sniffed carefully to nail down that scent. What was it? It seemed I had smelled it before . . .

"Dea, do you smell my cat?" asked Steffi.

Of course! She had a Precious of her own. That was unfortunate. This Steffi was a cat person, then. It was not a point in her favor, even though she clearly knew good petting techniques. I supposed I could forgive her in time.

Alison seemed to like Steffi, and I saw the danger that they might bond and then I'd have to sit through the whole female bonding ritual that could go on for hours, yap, yap, yap. They were already up to the part of the ritual where they complimented each other on this and that. I love your earrings. What a cute haircut. Come on, girls, sniff each other and get it over with. Then they started trotting out their life stories, with this one going to Rome and writing a book and that one growing up in Czechoslovakia and coming here many years ago and wanting to read the other one's book, and the other one offering to send her a copy. At least they kept petting me until I began to nod off. I was just starting to see the enemy *squirrel* take shape in front of me when I was rudely awakened from my siesta and made to slip and slide on the lobby tiles on the way back to our room.

I thought it was time for a cuddle in bed, but no, Alison put on the clothing she wears for the gym, and we went to a place where I had to sit inside my comfy bag and watch Alison run, run, run forever on a machine while going nowhere. How silly was that?

Back in the room, Alison started touching her foot a lot and saying, "Ow." I licked her toes, but she said the joint of her big toe was hurting. "It'll pass, monkey," she said, although I didn't hear much conviction in her voice.

This was not new. My Alison seemed to hurt something on her body every time she tried something new. Poor mama, I think all those internet dates with men who cannot bother themselves to wear shirts had made her nervous and clumsy. It was almost like when I shook my body so hard that I stumbled and fell. I knew that when it was cold out, she made me wear booties when I walked her, so maybe I should have started insisting that she wear special booties all the time to protect her. She cannot be trusted to make the slightest move without it ending in an "Ow."

I strained at the leash to walk Alison near the water again. It was so salty, and I could still smell a storm nearby, coming closer. When the first drops of rain began to fall, Alison insisted we go inside, which is crazy. When it rains it is time to splash in puddles and get mud all over. Why would she not want that?

Alison was feeling under the weather, which was also silly, because we are always under the weather. The weather is in the sky, and we are under it. But she ordered room service for dinner and wasn't even hungry. She left a big, moist, lovely, smelly piece of roasted chicken on her plate. She made the mistake of covering it with a metal dome, which prevented me from accessing this very tasty-smelling thing that was making me drool. The aroma was so intoxicating, I thought I might be hallucinating. From wanting that roasted chicken, I understood pain, believe me. That's why I could understand why Alison was in so much pain that she talked to the box with the cord and called it the front desk and asked the box for two Advil. She didn't say why she needed the Advil, but I suspected it was because the piece of roasted chicken was still under the metal dome, and it must have hurt her as deeply as it hurt me to leave it there. Maybe she forgot where she'd put it? Human noses don't work very well. Or maybe she was too weak to lift the metal dome after hurting her foot earlier?

"No, but I really need it," she said to the plastic box. "I understand your policies, but I can barely put any weight on one leg. . . . No, I can't go to the ER. I can't leave my dog here alone."

The ER is a room that is brightly lit and full of loud beeping sounds and where v-e-t people in white lab coats rush around like they can't find the exit. They are very busy, but not too busy to poke you if you happen to doze off. I know all this because Alison was able to take me along with her in my special zippered bag with the breathing mesh.

This was a big, wonderful adventure, so I don't know why my Alison's face leaked all the way there. We got to see our new friend Steffi again, who came by before the ambulance left to reassure us that she would look in on us in the morning and not to worry about a thing. Through the netting of the bag, I could see four human legs and four hairy arms as they put Alison on a bed with wheels, with me in my bag on top of Alison.

"*Ow!*" she screeched.

I have to admit, my Alison had been a little careless of late, often bumping into things. "First dates are stressful," she said. I told her those men spelled trouble. Now she was having accidents because of them.

I enjoyed being on the bed with wheels. I was right on top, so I was part of the action. They wheeled us into the ambulance, which is a truck that makes more noise than my squeakiest squeaky toy, but I put on my finest poodle behavior. I didn't utter a single grunt.

I can't say the same for my Alison, who made grunting sounds the whole way. I wanted to kiss away her pain at not being near the leftover piece of roasted chicken, but I was stuck inside the netted bag.

Once they transferred my mama onto a bigger bed with bigger wheels and put me in my bag on a chair where I could oversee the proceedings and make sure they took good care of her, it was time for the question-and-answer event. This is where a V-E-T comes around with a clipboard and asks the very same questions the last V-E-T with a clipboard asked.

"Please give me something for the pain," said Alison, her leaky face wet all over.

"Just a few more questions."

There was a scary eternity when they wheeled my mama into an X-ray room and I had to wait in my bag on a chair outside without my green blanket to give me the security I very much needed.

"Good news, sweet girl," she told me later. "Nothing's broken. But it sure feels like it is."

Yes, the pain of missing out on a perfectly good piece of roasted chicken is a deep, deep pain. It's a "ten" on the pain chart. Not everyone can tolerate it.

A few millennia later, a V-E-T came by with the next-best thing to roast chicken—pain pills. "I'll give you these now," he said. "Take the stronger one when you get back to your hotel."

Alison swallowed the pills with a fluted paper cup of water.

"Did you figure out the diagnosis?" she asked the V-E-T.

"Yes, it's pseudo gout," he said.

"Pardon?"

"Pseudo gout."

Alison was turning red, which was never a good sign.

"What do you mean, '*pseudo*'?" she said, almost as if the V-E-T had insulted her. "It hurts this bad, and I don't even get to have the real thing?"

"It *is* a real thing."

"But gout . . . even the pseudo kind . . . isn't that for big men who eat too much cheese and red meat? I don't even eat those things!"

"Pseudo gout calls for a different type of treatment, so you do need to get it checked out with your primary care," said the v-e-t. "And yes, it's still a painful condition."

Back in New York, Alison checked in with her primary care v-e-t, and when she told me the news, I was full of joy. The pain in her foot turned out to be arthritis with trauma to the joint. Wasn't that fantastic news? No pseudo anything for my mama, only the real thing!

As I fell asleep with my blue dinosaur in my mouth, I reflected on our marvelous adventure—new friends, humans with hairy arms, fishy scents by the water, rolling beds—and best of all, the relief of knowing that beneath a metal dome somewhere is a piece of roasted chicken with my name on it.

The Way to Inner Peace Is through Sniffing Others

Something was up. Alison gave me a brand-new stuffed toy, very unlike my others. Yes, I am an amazingly good poodle and deserve new toys, but my Alison had been acting strangely lately.

"Dea, this is a little Buddha stuffed toy for you," she said. "Look at his big, soft belly, monkey. Yes, that's right, go ahead and poke it with your nose."

I had to be careful poking anything because my nose had been feeling very sensitive. It kept twitching from an awful, bitter new smell pervading every nook and cranny of our home. It often made me sneeze, and when I sneeze, I shake all over and my hind legs shoot out behind me for a moment until I regain my balance. Sneezing always startled me, and I didn't appreciate losing my sense of poodle decorum.

For some reason, the putrid stench did not seem to bother my mama in the least. I even caught her sniffing it in deeply, using her open palm to waft it in toward her snout. Then she'd say, "Aah," and seemed a bit calmer. She seemed to believe the acrid smell contained healing powers.

She had also taken to opening a big book and smoothing the pages. She turned page after page and smoothed each one.

"The Buddha is important, sweet girl," she said.

Okay, I'll nose it a bit more in its big belly if it's all that important to you.

"It represents a whole new philosophy on life," she continued. "It's going to transform my outlook. More positive, less negative. The glass half full."

Personally, I was just fine with my outlook. The water bowl should not be half full; it should be full, period. I did not have to cultivate joy, because joy sprang eternal with each new sunrise and every time I saw my doggie friends in the park. We all got along super well. Very *simpatico*. I'd been taking Italian lessons on Skype with Alison.

"Are you enjoying the incense?" Alison asked me. "It's supposed to ground me and make me more attentive."

So *that* was the source of the noxious smell, incense, a magic potion designed to make humans calm down just enough to have what came naturally to dogs—an ability to feel so safe that we can fall asleep, drooling, with our tender bellies exposed and our paws pawing in the air while we dream of *squirrels*. You need a good attitude on life to get to that.

Alison apparently thought she could achieve doggie nirvana by opening a book called *Awakening the Buddha Within* and smoothing each page with her open palm while she turned them. The book was by a spiritual teacher named Lama Surya Das—and that just cracked me up every time! What kind of name was Lama? Isn't that an animal I once saw on the box at the foot of our bed, when it showed moving pictures from a zoo? Next thing I knew, Alison would be studying a book written by an elephant!

All this new nonsense in the house I could trace back to Ted, somehow. "I get too attached, monkey," said Alison. "It's a problem I need to fix."

This alarmed me, because I did not want her becoming too attached to my toys. They are *my* toys, and I am already attached to them, especially the red lobster.

"The Lama says we need to stop lingering in the past and trying to figure out the future when we could be living in the present moment," said Alison as she smoothed another page of the book by the zoo animal. "He also says to be honest with who you are and not to be self-deceiving."

Well, that's very interesting about people not being able to live in the present, but . . . oh, wait! She's getting up to get me a *cookie*! I am not a self-deceiving poodle. I know what I need and what I want.

"My heartache and suffering comes from an old place," said Alison when she resumed smoothing her pages. "My attachment to Ted was only partly about him, but mostly about old things that happened, about my parents divorcing and how they separated me from my father and sister and brother, and about people I loved dying. It all makes me feel dependent on others. It makes me lose sight of who I am."

That sounded very sad, but her book had a happy ending. The zoo animal said attachment could also be a good thing. It could be pure and filled with love, just like her attachment with *me*. What we have together is bowwow perfect. There, problem solved!

Except that Alison still did not quite get it.

"I need to look deep inside myself for answers to my struggles and not look outward to other people to solve them for me," she said.

Okay, sure! So, let's move on and you throw the red lobster and I'll fetch it. I will look within to see if I'm hungry yet. Oh, I think I am!

"I cannot rely on new romantic interests like the Italian guy who moved to Italy to make me feel whole and fulfilled."

Great! Good insight! Now let's eat a chicken treat.

"I need to learn to meditate to instill a deepening of my life's meaning."

Well, duh! Let's go outdoors and play!

"It's going to take time," she said, ignoring my wise suggestions. "It's a practice. It's a training."

Mama, I know all about training! I'll fill you in. Now, let's move on.

But no, she smoothed some more pages, she sniffed in some more odiferous smoke, she counted her breaths. This was going nowhere.

"Sweet girl, I need to read all about death and dying, because I have a huge fear of it," she said.

Hey, all the more reason *not* to read about that! I never worried about my own death, because I was a glorious poodle and planned to live forever. Also, I needed to be here for my Alison because she clearly could not cope without me. Who would be there to walk her if I were gone?

"My father died when he was fifty-seven," she said. "My brother, David, died when he had just turned sixty-three, even before my mother died when she was eighty-nine. My friend and surrogate mother Grace died, and although she was ninety and she lived a full life, I feel like people are ripped from me too early. I'm afraid to love, for fear of losing them, and I'm afraid *not* to love, for fear of being adrift in a lonely universe."

Snooze. I love the sound of Alison's voice, but the stories in the animal's book were lulling me to sleep.

I was just dozing off on Alison's lap, feeling totally safe and sleepy-eyed, when she startled me awake with some more yapping from the animal book.

"The Lama discusses that Buddhism accepts death as a natural part of life, because life is ephemeral, you know, temporary, and understanding this is important for a person's well-being. It helps us to not take life for granted. All we have is this moment in the here and now, so it doesn't make sense to worry about what we don't know. What do you think, Dea? I think that's so true! Each time I came home from the hospital after my cancer surgeries, I really did appreciate life better, at least for a while. Illness like that attunes you to impermanence and makes you cherish each moment. But that feeling fades, or it did for me. I need to learn how to hold onto it and no longer fear death and loss. If I accept that I can die at any time, like anyone, then maybe I can live my life more fully."

I tell you what, mama, if we went to the park right now and you tossed a stick for me, you would forget all this nonsense, and you would live your life to the max, I guarantee it.

"I will try to focus on the things that are most important and meaningful and not on the small, meaningless stuff."

Bingo! But it was clearly a moment to take action, and by action I did not mean turning a bunch of pages. I whimpered and made it quite clear that it was time for me to walk Alison. She talked about using her eyes to become a more observant person in the universe that we all share, and I allowed her to blather on like that all the way in the noisy elevator box on the way to the lobby.

"Because he says that when we see clearly, we discover we have all that we really need and can give up our illusions . . ."

You said it, lady. All I need is you and my dog friends and a few chicken treats. I'm very into the simple pleasures of life.

"And if I can give up my expectations of others, I won't be so disappointed and sad all the time."

I had expectations, too, and I expected to get what I wanted—a lovely, blood-pounding, life-affirming jaunt in the park, full of sniffing and grass beneath my paws and tussling with my buddies and getting our leashes entwined. An afternoon of frolic in the sun and a glass half full and *squirrels* just begging me to chase them. You said nothing is permanent in life? I beg to disagree! And I certainly do know how to beg. What was permanent and unchanging was that every day was a wonderful new adventure. Looked like I'd been a Buddhist all along.

Outside, I pulled on the leash as hard as I could. Clearly, it was important to get Alison to move around and take all that energy out of her head and into her blood.

We ran into Iggy outside in the park. He squealed from a distance when he saw me and pulled Delia over to say hello. He sniffed me top to toe, or rather nose to rump, and gave Alison a slurpy kiss on her cheek.

"Sorry, can't stay long," said Delia. "I'm watching Stella's baby today while she's at work."

But even a moment with Iggy always brightened my day.

As we progressed farther into the park, I sniffed a new white, fluffy dog who was a bit uppity for my tastes. She didn't even have the courtesy to sniff my behind, which demonstrated an enormous breach of protocol and lack of breeding. I shook it off because life is full of travesties like this, and the important thing is to carry on and treasure your real friends, your true friends, the friends who will never fail to sniff your behind.

If only Alison sniffed her friends head to butt, she would be so much happier and Zen-like.

When we got back home, I was still leaping and bounding with excitement, but Alison had already forgotten her training.

"Did you know that we are all interconnected in life?" she asked me. "We are all joined and brought together simply by the air we breathe. That's what the book says."

Oh, brother. Here we go again.

"Dea, I want to try and find a way to feel more complete. To live in the present and not ruminate on past thoughts or attempt to guess what's coming next. I need help with this. I'm going to try meditation."

I soon learned what this thing called meditation was. It's when you sit still and listen to a voice from a little box telling you to sit even *more* still, and then you think of a list of things you want to do, and the voice in the little box tells you to stop thinking about that, and you jiggle your foot and then remember not to jiggle anything, and then you think of how *other* people manage not to jiggle their feet and how much better at meditation they are and how you are hopeless at it, and then you steal a look at the clock. All while doing this, there is stinky incense burning and making your nose tickle. Every now and then there is a booming gong sound that makes you jump out of your skin. I could not see how any of this was going to help my Alison live in the present and forget about Ted and find it in her heart to give me peanut butter.

"I must not get bogged down with excess baggage," said Alison as she shifted her position yet again. "We must wake up from within. Become alert to ourselves."

But the Buddha was wrong on this, and so was the man with the animal name. We did not need to wake up from within, not after a really wonderful yet tiring walk in the park. We needed to snooze.

I curled up on Alison's lap and nudged my head beneath her hand.

"I want to reflect more on things I have done," murmured Alison. "I'd like to make more friends. I would like to find love again. I need to feel and show gratitude."

What you need to do, mama, is pet me and give a big sigh, like this. See how I did that? And now close your eyes and breathe evenly, in and out, in and out, and start thinking of *squirrels*. Yes, *squirrels*. With their beady little eyes and stupid darting tails as they clutch their nuts and sit on *our* bench, the one where we should be sitting and they should not.

I nuzzled closer, with my nose in Alison's face. The little box stopped disturbing us with gongs and played soft chimes. I could feel my mama's heartbeat. It felt warm and safe. After a few minutes, we were breathing in harmony. We were completely connected.

We continued listening to the little man inside the box each afternoon as the light outside turned golden.

Heart and Soul

My Alison's throwing ability had been off since breakfast. She kept clutching her left side.

"Sorry, monkey, I know that was bad," she apologized after a particularly weak attempt.

I'll say. She usually throws my favorite toy of the day all the way down the hall, and this time the black-and-white dragon only made it halfway before I went to fetch it back.

I knew just what to do to get her back in top throwing form. I pretended to leave the toy by her feet, but right before she bent to pick it up, I grabbed it and trotted off, playing the flirt. Usually, she loved this and would laugh, but this time she looked away and sighed.

This was highly puzzling. Had I lost my super poodle powers? I tried a few more antics and still got no response. She continued to touch and gently massage the left side of her chest while she gave me my breakfast. What was she hiding there? Was it a *cookie*?

I was still demolishing my breakfast when my ears pitched upward. I could hear her talking to the box with the curly cord. Was she female bonding this early in the morning? That was not our usual routine.

"Yes, in the rib area, the same side as the last cancer," she was telling the box.

I took her for a long walk, but she was holding my leash with the wrong hand, so I tried to walk nicely without zigzagging and pulling her too much. I can be a very understanding poodle. I focused on two ducks that had waddled out of the river and into the park, clearly for my sole entertainment. I wondered what their fat, plucky bodies would feel like beneath my paw. I stared at their long duck snouts. This was a rare, up-close sighting, and I couldn't wait to tell all my dog pals, but Alison didn't seem to recognize the enormity of this encounter. But mama, they looked right at me! With their silly duck faces! I had to admit I was a little miffed that they did not cower in fear at the sight of me. I have shoulders of steel from pulling on my leash all the time. Did they not know I am a mighty swimmer? A little respect.

The plastic box with the cord was making a ringing sound when we walked in the door, and Alison hurtled over to talk at it.

"It's been a few days and it's very painful. . . . A bag of frozen peas? Yes, I have that. . . . Okay, I'll try it and let you know," she said.

She went into the wee-wee-pad room and rummaged inside the big box that made my nose super cold when I touched it. She took out a lumpy bag with pictures of peas on it and placed it on her chest. After a bit, she put it back in the cold box, and then she took it out again and put it on her chest. My Alison is a sweet angel, but she cannot seem to make up her mind, and if there were actual peas inside that bag, they were meant for me to eat, mashed together with other yummy foods.

The stress of having to decide whether to take the lumpy bag out of the cold box or put it back in must have taken a toll on her, because she grew listless during the day and her body began to shake slightly. I gave her a close snuggle. It worried me when she got agitated like this. She is my world, and I am her sun.

We lay in bed watching the screen with moving pictures when the box with the cord made the ringing sound. "Maybe it's the nurse again," said Alison, jumping up, just when I had been so comfy with my nose on her tummy. She had to hold the box with one hand and the cold lumpy bag with the other, so she pressed the magic button and the box spoke.

"Hi, it's Margarita again, Dr. Jacobs's nurse practitioner," said the box. "I hope I didn't wake you, but I wanted to check in and see if you're feeling any better."

"I've been using the frozen peas on and off, like you said, but it hasn't helped at all," said Alison. "If anything, the pain is worse."

"We think, after a lot of consideration, that you need to come into our urgent care center."

I could sense Alison's body getting very rigid.

"But why?" she asked, her voice strangled. "What do you think it is?"

"We just want to make sure that your heart isn't involved."

"My *heart?*"

"We really would like you to come in tonight, if you can."

"No, I can't!" said Alison. "I have my dog to take care of. Can't it wait until tomorrow morning?"

"Is there someone who can watch your dog for you?" asked Margarita. "We'd really prefer you come in now."

Alison clicked off the box and paced around the living room. I didn't like the vibe she was giving off. It was as if a terrible thunder cloud had descended over everything. I followed her around, my tail hanging straight as if weights were pulling it down. It did not make me feel better that she began talking to the plastic box and, one by one, calling it the name of each of her friends.

"Nina, sorry to call so late, but I need to know your opinion . . ."

"Michael, my oncologist thinks I should go in tonight . . ."

The box did not cheer her up. She decided she could not leave me during the night and go to this urgent care v-e-t, and even though I was always happy to have her by my side, I wondered whether she should have gone after all, whether it would have made her feel better. They would have a much better cold, lumpy bag to give her, the kind experts use—no doubt colder and lumpier.

"Sweet girl, I'm afraid . . .," she said before we fell asleep, not finishing her sentence. What was she afraid of? Was she afraid she would run out of cold bags of peas? Was she afraid she would not be able to throw my morning toy far enough?

She woke me way too early the next morning. I have a routine, and this was not part of it. She knew that I liked to get up at 7:30 a.m. and not one minute before. I need my poodle beauty sleep so I can attract Gerard, the white, fluffy standard poodle. He's a real looker, and his scent back there is marvelous.

She fed me my breakfast too early as well, and that made me confused, and I was still groggy, so she sat on the floor next to my bowl of kibble and hand-fed me until I finished. She had not hand-fed me since I was a tiny yet mighty-in-personality puppy. It was pleasant to be hand-fed, but it was not part of the approved routine. Have I mentioned how much I like having a routine?

With my schedule all twisted around, I have to admit I was a bit nervous and grumpy. I was not happy to hear I would have to go babysit Sue for the day, and maybe longer, depending on when Alison got back from the urgent care V-E-T. I did not feel like dealing with Precious and her green-blanket-stealing ways.

I knew Alison was involved in something major and had many things on her mind, but she had no idea what horrors I had to face that day while she went for an X-ray. An X-ray is a photo that shows the inside instead of the outside. I know this because I had one once. It was when I was just a few months old, and I jumped up higher than the moon to show off my incredible jumping skills and landed too hard on my hind leg. It caused my kneecap to move out of place—a "luxating patella," according to Alison. "It's a trick knee," she said, although this wasn't a fun trick that made anyone laugh.

She said I was born this way, so it wasn't my fault, but I wasn't proud that I shrieked like a baby. Alison rushed me to the V-E-T, where they gave me an X-ray, and then the people in white lab coats pretended it was a book and they "read" it.

"We read the X-ray," they told Alison. Why they had to waste time reading when I was in so much pain, I cannot tell you. Strange are the ways of humans.

Reading my X-rays must have put them in a very bad mood, because they made me swallow some nasty-tasting pills. At home, Alison tried to hide the pills inside a special soft *cookie*. I didn't want to embarrass her by letting her know how bad she was at trying to trick me, so I pretended I didn't realize the nasty pills were inside the *cookie*—when, come on, I saw her put them in there, and I could smell the nastiness of the pill right through the cookie layer—so I gobbled it down and smacked my lips just to make her feel better about herself.

So, while Alison got an X-ray, I had no choice but to babysit the hopeless Sue while Precious walked around me in a circle and disgustingly rubbed her stupid white fur all over me. She headbutted me softly. What nerve! It was intolerable. And then—I am ashamed even to admit this—she did something so awful, there are no words to describe it.

She licked me!

I don't know if she realized or could even comprehend that I go to a professional groomer when I need something like that. The groomer shampoos me and hoses me down and blow-dries me and trims my nails and gives me a *cookie*. I did not need nasty cat saliva all over my carefully groomed and very dignified self. You can bet I would be reporting this to the authorities.

"Aww, look at the two of you," crooned Sue, but she did not know what she was talking about.

Precious continued to lap at me with her sandpaper tongue. I woofed a little to tell her this was not the least bit cool, but she seemed intent on this freakish preoccupation of hers. I'm tough and a survivor, so I withstood the icky onslaught.

Fortunately, I did not have to stay overnight in that hellish place, with a cat licking me and purring at me and generally making my life miserable. Alison picked me up and took me home, and I was so grateful I kissed her all over.

"They don't know what it is," she told the box with the cord. "They said maybe a contusion or a trauma there, but nothing has happened to me lately. I haven't fallen; I didn't hurt it."

This all sounded like good news to me. I reached up with my hind leg to scratch behind my ear and get rid of any lingering residue of that foul cat licking me. Alison was home. We were both safe. Everything was fine and always would be, forever and ever.

125

Scanning for Pets

A lison's cancer doctor was inside the white plastic box with the cord. I knew this because Alison pressed the magic button, and I could hear the tiny voice. There were so many little people inside that box.

"I want you to have a PET scan," came the doctor's voice. "It's the best way to know what's going on."

"A what?"

"A PET scan."

It sounded good to me, since I am Alison's pet, after all, and I didn't mind some scanning if it would make her calm down a bit. She'd been quite frazzled since she first had that new pain and the X-ray never figured it out.

"A PET scan is . . .," the oncologist's voice said, but Alison cut her off.

"I know exactly what it is," she told the box. "I'm sorry, but I'll do any other test you think will help, but not a PET scan. Please don't ask me."

The tiny little oncologist's voice sounded puzzled as she asked and probed, and Alison began to leak and told the box the short version of a story I had heard several times. I could tell that v-e-t a thing or two.

For starters, in case you are not as medically aware as I have become with the help of Alison, a PET scan is a procedure at the v-e-t that looks inside you and does not hurt, but it makes you die. I don't know why it does not hurt and then it goes ahead and kills you anyway, but that is what happened to Alison's mother, and whenever Alison thought back to that time, she began to leak. Not all the poodle loving and nonstop kisses in the world could stop it.

Her mother had been beautiful, with dark hair and deep-set green eyes. Even when she got older and let her hair turn into silver streaks, it looked so stylish that people thought she'd had the hairdresser color it. She remained regal in manner, with her perfect pearls and impeccably matched outfits.

At seventy-nine, her mother received a diagnosis of breast cancer. She had been so focused on caring for her second husband, George, after his stroke that she didn't get herself checked up until the cancer was too far gone. Even then, she didn't tell Alison about it. She only told David and Deane. Alison feared that if the end was near, this might have cut short the remaining time she had with her mother.

"But why didn't you tell me?" Alison asked, leaking all over the place, when she finally found out.

"You're my sensitive girl. I didn't want to upset you," her mother said.

Alison's mother had the cancer removed, and Alison had nine more years in which to keep up her go-to technique of denial. But after nine years, the v-e-t called her mother in to have a PET scan.

"The test found that the cancer had spread to her bones," she told the oncologist who resided in Alison's plastic box with the cord. "A short time later, she died, and I was an orphan. She had been my only real parent, and now she was gone, and it was right after I lost my brother."

The oncologist's tiny little voice in the box made soft sounds of understanding and reassurance, but when she tried to explain that it might be better to know and potentially have the worry taken away if everything was good, Alison got even leakier and her voice got harder and louder.

"No, no, no," she insisted. "I don't want history repeating itself. Give me any other test, but not this one."

No one could argue with her. No one could reason with her. My Alison agreed to a CT scan instead, which would not scan for pets or any other kinds of animals.

I took her out for a long walk before the scan that would not look for any pets. Dogs have an innate ability to sense stress and nervousness, and my Alison had both of these. I could smell it on her skin and on her breath, and I could see it in her eyes and feel it in the way she jerked the leash. I tried to be obedient and not cause my Alison any extra stress, but when I saw Gus, I just had to pull and pull on the leash, and who could blame me? He's a doodle of some kind who lives in our building, with silky gray and black hair and a sweet disposition. Even Alison says Gus is the Cary Grant of dogs—although Cary Grant is really the Gus of humans, I had to remind her.

Gus was out walking his people, Tom and Greg. Gus had recently been to the groomer, so his behind didn't really have anything worth sniffing, but I sniffed anyway because I am a polite poodle and like to pay my respects. Even after the groomer, his scent was divine.

Later, Alison's friend Nina came over to go with her to the v-e-t for the nonPET scan. I bravely stayed home, the corner of my green blanket in my mouth for comfort.

When Alison came home again, I was ecstatic, but she barely threw my star toy that sounded like a squeaky trombone and closed herself up in our bedroom without me. What had I done wrong? Should we have played with a different toy with a different squeaky sound? I lay on the floor outside our room, trying to send good wishes through the slit beneath the door.

We both needed a *cookie* after that, but even with a *cookie*, Alison was not herself. She leaked a lot and kept getting distracted and didn't pay the right amount of attention to me. The right amount is undivided attention 24/7, as long as you asked.

I licked the salty wetness off her face to help her clean up while she held me in her arms like she had the first day we met at the breeder's house. She squeezed me a little too hard, but I am not a helpless puppy anymore. I am a robust thirteen-and-a-half-pound poodle. I can handle anything.

Alison did not feel better over the next few days. Her throwing of my toys was lackluster. Her face leaked. She talked to the plastic box nonstop, calling it the names of all her friends and telling it that waiting for the results of her test was "a killer." A lot of things were very murderous these days. I was picking up on the aura of fear myself and feeling a little shaky.

"Why don't you talk to a social worker?" the plastic box asked her after she pushed the magic button.

Alison agreed with the plastic box that this was a good idea. She pushed the magic button so she could hear the voices inside while she held me with one arm and held a box of tissues with the other.

The social worker who lived inside the little white box with the cord had a lot to say to Alison. "No matter what the outcome of your test, you must take care of yourself," she said.

"But what if I have a metastasis?" asked Alison. A metastasis is a bad thing, whatever it is. "In that case, I don't know what I'd do."

"You must focus on good things, happier things," said the tiny social worker in the box. "Do you meditate?"

"Yes, I've been doing that with my dog. It's helpful, but only to an extent. I feel this existential terror . . ."

Alison held me tightly while she leaked and talked. The tiny social worker was patient and kind.

"Trust in yourself that you have the ability to handle things, no matter what the test results show. You've already been through a lot, so you know what to do. Is there anyone else in your family to help?"

"Only my dog, Dea. She's my family. But what will happen to her if . . ."

Alison began to leak so hard that she couldn't talk anymore.

"Let's not jump ahead to conclusions," said the tiny social worker. "Even if there's a metastasis, you know that people can live a lot longer than they used to. There are medications . . ."

"But I'm only in my fifties!" wailed Alison. "This is not supposed to happen!"

The next day, Alison gave me a frozen KONG with some yogurt and banana and a taste of peanut butter, just like she did when I was a tiny puppy.

"I'm going in to get my results," she told me. "I'll be back before you know it."

I didn't understand what that meant. How could I know something before I knew it? I was still pondering that when I realized she had left me, probably forever. I really needed that green blanket now.

She finally returned after centuries had passed. She seemed a little distant. Although she threw a toy for me, she did not seem really into it.

She picked up the white plastic box with the cord and spoke to it. "A sclerosis, possibly being a benign osseous lesion, but metastasis cannot be excluded—particularly in the setting of rib pain," she said in a monotone, partly reading off a piece of paper she clutched along with a soggy Kleenex.

She read the piece of paper again and again to the plastic box, calling it by the names of all her friends, one by one.

At long last, she paid attention to me.

"Dea, I need to lie down," she said. "Will you lie there with me?"

Will I ever!

As we lay there together on the big bed, I felt an odd vibration. My Alison was trembling. I inched my way closer to her to warm her up.

"Dea, my monkey, I may be in trouble," she said. "I'm not sure I have the tools to get through this."

I'm here, mama.

And then she said something her brother, David, had always said to her, and although I liked her saying it to me, it made me very worried.

"I love you completely, little one," she said.

That's what David had said to her before he died.

Banging the Drum
for Alison

A lison needed to get out. Maybe she didn't know this, but I surely did. Now? How about now? I pleaded with my dark, chocolate-brown eyes.

All I could think of to get Alison up from the couch was to bring her my leash. I had never done that before, but as the brainy poodle I am, I snatched it from where it was dangling near the door and trotted it over to her. Now you can see why poodles are the second most intelligent canine breed after border collies, although I still don't know what border collies bring to the party. If I hear about them herding one more time, I'm really going to have to put my paw down.

Alison got the hint and gave a wan smile. She dragged herself to the door and out we went.

It was a good thing, too, because there was a block party outside with some of my canine friends and many all-new, intoxicating smells to inhale. I didn't know what to sniff first. They had set up a table inside the park with a big plate of twisty noodles and some other dishes, but the noodle plate had a really penetrating aroma.

"Pesto," said Alison. "Sorry, sweet girl, that's not for you in any case. It has garlic, basil, and pine nuts, but garlic is toxic to dogs, like chocolate." Fine. Be that way. There were plenty of other things to tickle my sensitive, quivering nose. There was corn on the cob, long and yellow. If only I could have one, my choppers would get a real workout, but these people were very rude, very inhospitable, and did not toss me a single one.

The best scent of all—one that nearly made me trip over myself—came from one particular platter. It was an answer to all my doggie prayers, or most of them, because I could tell with canine precision that it contained roasted chicken.

It was Gerard's birthday, the standard white poodle. "Maybe the party is just for him and his friends," said Alison. But I am Gerard's friend, too, and therefore entitled to some corn on the cob and roasted chicken, am I not? There were plenty of passerby dogs who had not earned the right to eat at Gerard's table, and yet they were crashing the party! I tugged Alison to let me join the party. She could not resist me and my wonderful, innate sense of GPS. I knew the way right to Gerard's nose, upon which I bestowed a particularly sloppy smooch. He was wearing a red birthday hat so no one could mistake just who was the birthday boy around these parts!

Parties are places for red hats, good smells, and new friends. I met Kayla, a sweet dachshund who became totally submissive the minute I approached. She set down the toy rabbit she had been carrying so proudly in her mouth and rolled over to expose her belly. How gracious of her! We sniffed and play-bowed and woofed happily.

Maxwell's human, Angie, tried to interact with Alison, but my Alison apologized and said she didn't have much energy these days. It was also my first time meeting Maxwell, a mixed-breed cross between a bloodhound and some kind of terrier. He was so busy sniffing the ground thoroughly that he didn't notice when we left.

Well, I had energy enough for two. I immediately turned on my coy behavior as befits a drama queen like *moi*. The block party was chockablock with four-legged friends, but I pretended not to notice Herbie, the white Maltese who had a crush on both me and Alison. Herbie looked like he would faint with delight when he saw us, but instead of acknowledging him, I sniffed hello to Cody, a fat, lumbering pit bull with the sweetest disposition, a real Miss Congeniality. I was really getting my flirt on, and it drove Herbie crazy, to the point where he practically tripped Bruna, his human, in his rush to get my attention.

"Herbie!" Bruna admonished him in a tone of voice that sounded more like she was saying, "Everything you do is so adorable, Herbie!"

Alison bent down stiffly to pet Herbie. She liked Bruna, too, but she didn't pet her. Once again, humans have the most self-defeating habits. I don't know how they would have survived evolution without dogs befriending them and showing them how to love.

Herbie made an attempt to hump me, but Alison quickly put a stop to that, while Bruna once again said, "Herbie!" in a tone of voice that said, "Go ahead and hump anyone all you like, since you're so cute!"

We made our way along the block party, stopping every time I met a friend or just another dog who needed sniffing. We ran into Reggie, or he ran into us—that's the golden retriever puppy who lives in our building and is so obsessed with my butt I have to give him a slap every now and then. Clearly, he was vying with me for the title of Best Drama Queen, because he fell to the ground and rolled onto his back with his paws hanging uselessly in the air in a pathetic attempt to get Alison to rub his belly. Shameless. His human, Nellie, just laughed while giving me a quick pet on my back.

At least it got Alison to laugh, the first time I'd heard her laugh in a while. "Thanks, monkey. It's good to get out," she said.

I was proud that it was my intelligent thinking about bringing her the leash that gave her this moment where she could relax. That is my colossal poodle power.

It wasn't long afterward that Alison began using her hurting arm to throw my toys in the morning. "You know, monkey, I think the pain is better," she told me. "The truth is, I just didn't want to know whatever that PET scan would have shown. The doctor will keep an eye on me, but sometimes life is easier when you simply let go and move on. I know other people would want to know, but I just couldn't handle it. I couldn't. So, we move forward. I choose to move forward. That part, at least, is in my control."

I was still concerned for my Alison that she didn't do what the v-e-t wanted her to do, but I know all about moving forward. That's what I had to do the time a cute Lhasa Apso with flowing white hair rejected me. She had a waterfall of hair, so much that I had trouble locating her snout. The allure of her new scent was intoxicating, but as soon as I came close, she barked at me. The nerve! She even tried to snap at me. I was shocked. It was hurtful to my poodle pride, but I am letting it go. I choose to move forward. Anyway, it's really her loss and she will regret it until the day she crosses the Rainbow Bridge.

At least Alison seemed to be feeling better. She showed interest again in the book she had written about living in Rome, the land of long, and occasionally curly, noodles. The best part of the book is the very end, when I make an appearance.

Alison began paying more attention to her online Italian lessons with her teacher, Daniela, overseas. I sat on Alison's lap while she made these musical Italian words and Daniela corrected her. It reminded me of when I learned to sit and stay and roll over, except I can tell you I am a much faster learner than Alison. The human brain does not take direction very well, at least not when the human is ancient, like most of the people I see on our walks in the park. They're all rather old, and, poor things, they can no longer learn new tricks.

In case you're wondering what it's like to learn Italian, it goes like this: The teacher greets me with gusto, saying my full name with a lot of flair. Dea Della Vita, goddess of life. Then there's a lot of yap, yap, yap, and then the more important stuff happens when the teacher again says my full name and tells me how good and how beautiful I am, how I am *fantastico, bellissima*, which is all true. She blows me kisses. I kiss Alison and I kiss the screen, and the lesson is over.

Now that Alison was thinking about *A Place Called Grace* again and taking more Italian lessons, she decided she needed to get some more reviews of her book. That would encourage other people to buy it, she said.

"I need to hire a publicist," she told me. "Someone to trumpet my accomplishments."

I knew I could help with the trumpeting because I have my star-shaped toy that sounds like a trombone when you squeeze it. We have all the musical instruments we need to help Alison sell her book.

Alison took me to see Sally, someone who could lead the orchestra of these musical instruments to "bang the drum" for Alison's book, as she said. When we rang the doorbell, we heard dogs barking from somewhere inside, which was certainly a sign that this Sally was very professional and knew just what she was doing. Could life get any better?

Sally had a warm smile and a big personality, just like me, but not as much hair as I do. She would not last long at the groomer, but she was an okay person anyway. She had two trembling chihuahuas who were cowering under a bed and clearly needed protection from bullies.

After Sally—a veteran publicist in her late seventies, but who looked much younger—said more about what she did, I began to understand that publicity is not just about banging drums and blowing trumpets. It is about making people read all about *moi*. That is what a book publicist does—gets other people to know my story, even if I only appeared on one or two pages way at the end of Alison's book. Still, it is a worthy profession, this publicity thing.

"My dream is to have a book signing," said Alison. "Do you think you can help?"

"There are no guarantees," said Sally. "It's a tough market, selling books. But we'll certainly work on that, and it's very important to do a reading and signing if you want to sell copies,"

"Can we get some good reviews on Amazon?"

Amazon is a place "online"—not the same place as where the men are too warm to wear their shirts, but maybe it's nearby. It's a place where you look at pictures of things and start salivating, even when it's not pictures of food, and you go into a kind of coma like with the box of moving pictures, and while you are deep in this salivating coma, you start sending it money. Then you wake up the next morning, and there are packages at your door of things you don't remember buying.

They made a deal, and Sally said she'd get right on it. Things were starting to happen.

And then *too many* things started to happen—Alison got it into her head that she should return to Italy. Without me.

"Janie, I'm in need of a break! I've been having quite a time, and not in the good sense."

Alison was talking to the plastic box with the cord and calling it Janie, the person who had saved Alison's bacon. As a reminder, a break is what you take before you explode, but last time Alison needed one, she took me along. This time, she had the total wrong idea.

She got very excited about planning this horrible non-Dea trip. I was glad she was no longer leaking while clutching her side in pain, but this was a poor substitute, and Janie was no help. The girl was constantly encouraging my Alison to do it, to make the trip, to abandon me until the cows came home, and you know they never do.

"I showed your book to the bookstore here that you like, the Anglo-American one," said Janie inside the box after Alison pushed the magic button.

"You did?" Alison squealed that last word right into my eardrum. I had to reposition myself on her lap or I'd go deaf.

"I told them it mostly takes place in Rome, so they're ordering some copies. You can do a reading here!"

"Oh, no!" Alison said.

"What do you mean 'oh, no'? This is great news. Isn't this what you wanted?"

"Yes, but . . . they're going to hate it!"

"Why do you say that?"

Alison went on with her same old glass-half-empty delirium. I'd heard her like this before, ranting about how nothing would ever go well for her, and I usually tuned it out and waited for the next time we meditated.

"They're going to rip out the pages and use them for firewood!" said Alison, grabbing the Drama Queen crown away from both me and Reggie, the golden retriever, without even a by-your-leave.

"Don't sell yourself short," said Janie. "They're going to love it."

You know who wasn't loving it? Me. Little old me, babysitting Sue once again, putting up with the awful snowball cat who slept in the most ridiculous positions and gave me the most baleful stares. Always plotting and scheming for world dominance. Always lick, lick, licking her stupid fur and then trying to lick my face when she ran out of her own body parts to clean. The things I put up with for my Alison.

When Alison reappeared again one day, I wasn't sure she'd remember me, so I reminded her by yelping, running round and round in circles, and kissing her until she couldn't breathe because she was laughing so hard. She took me home, where she gave me treats, rubbed my belly, cooed my name a lot, and told me all about her non-Dea trip to Italy.

"I saw all my old friends there," she said. If they were old, maybe they shouldn't have been trying to learn Italian, but she said they all spoke Italian just fine. "I saw Janie every day for lunch. I went to Francesco's for dinner. He still has an amazing voice and can sound just like Frank Sinatra, but with an Italian accent! And his wife, Elisabetta, prepared a feast for us."

My mouth was watering already, but Alison was selfish and had not brought back any curly noodles with *cheese* for me from Italy. I had put up with Precious, I had listened to that feline's foul rumbling like an engine from deep inside her chest, and no noodles with *cheese* for me. What is this world coming to?

At least my Alison was back to normal, throwing toys for me down the little hallway to increase my voluminous appetite for mealtime and bubbling over with stories of her friends in Italy and her first book signing ever. Apparently, no one tore the pages out and used them for firewood after all.

"All my friends came. Janie; Francesco and Elisabetta and their daughter, Carla; Daniela—you know her, our Italian teacher—and Vince, my cousin Jody's husband, who just happened to be visiting Rome at that time."

For those of you not in the know about the publishing world the way I am, a book reading is a public event where you get so nervous beforehand you want to barf, but your friends push you to do it anyway because they think it will be good for you, and you're so angry with your friends you want to kill them for making you go through this horrible ordeal. When the day of the event finally comes, you're sorry you chose that particular outfit to wear because it makes you look fat or a million years older, and you're sure no one will come—because, come on, why would they?—and you can't believe you ever wrote a book in the first place if it was going to come to this, and you hate the day you were born.

The next step in this process is when the reading actually happens. Lots of people show up with smiles and applause. and you feel like you own the world. You wonder why you didn't do this sooner. People buy your book and want you to sign it like you're someone special, and your friends buy you drinks afterward, and the world is a lovely place full of indescribable pleasures.

Yes, that is what a book reading is.

Darkness This Way Comes

Alison loved doing book readings and book signings. People listened to what she had to say and said they could relate to her story. I was on the brink of becoming a very famous black poodle.

She had also done a hike while she was in Sicily, and that seemed to awaken her old passion for taking long walks and going uphill, which was something I was very good at, too, with my robust thigh muscles and sturdy paws. She said the like-minded group she thought she'd be hiking with in Italy never showed, but she drank in the wonders of nature with her handsome Italian guide, Lorenzo. I don't know how she drank that in without taking a water bowl along, but somehow, she managed.

I wondered whether she'd bumped into that mean Italian guy she had dated once, who fled to Italy and never came back, but Alison says it is a very big place, this land of twisty noodles, and you can hike a long time without seeing another soul, let alone one who stirs up unpleasant memories.

Now our lives were very full—we went hiking, we played up to three times a day, and we visited Sally a lot to discuss more opportunities to bang the drum and trumpet my literary debut. The chihuahuas always hid beneath a piece of furniture, shivering. I thought they should go to that "online" place with the men who were too warm to put on shirts, that maybe they'd be more comfortable in that kind of temperature, but every time I tried to make one-on-one contact with their muzzles, they backed even further under the furniture and shivered some more. Those dogs need coats, if you ask me. I have several coats, and the weather had been getting cool enough for me to wear them sometimes, but mine are too big for these little chihuahuas. Also, I don't think they could possibly pull off a fashion statement the way I do. I am a real fashionista. My wardrobe makes Alison chuckle with admiration.

For example, I have a new gold-colored puffer jacket. It's very puffy and covers my slim torso and barrel chest. Also in my wardrobe is a pink-and-purple-striped turtleneck sweater. Alison's mother used to say poodles look spectacular in turtlenecks because of their long necks, so I guess I have her to thank for this addition to my closet, even though I never met her.

I also have a yellow raincoat with a hood and two cool pockets for treats. And I still have the jacket Ted gave me, but I don't wear it because when I do, Alison's face gets all scrunched up.

The only part of my wardrobe I'm not keen on are the red balloon booties. I don't like when Alison tries to get them on over my pedicured paws. They often get stuck going over the sharp nails of my lovely dew-claws, but my Alison doesn't give up. She gives it the old college try, even though I'm not sure red balloon booties are the quite dignified look I'm after.

At least I have things that keep me warm all the time. These two chihuahuas look like they would freeze into nervous little blocks of ice if they went outdoors even once.

People generally admire my elegant wardrobe while I'm taking Alison for a walk, but there are always a few bad apples. There was one man who had been petting an Irish setter, and although I waited patiently for him to forget the setter and turn his attention to me, he pointedly ignored me. "I prefer them larger," he sniffed to Alison. "I don't think of poodles as real dogs."

What can I say? Haters gonna hate. I can run circles around an Irish setter. Poodles are one of the most athletic canines out there, so he and his Irish setter can go sit on a broken bench, for all I care.

"I've gotten you a signing at a nice bookstore in Brooklyn," said Sally. "Don't worry, I'll go with you."

Alison did one of those shouts that busts the eardrum, so I jumped off her lap and went foraging for treats, which the chihuahuas sometimes left abandoned on the floor in their haste to hide beneath an article of furniture so they can palpitate in private. I don't think Alison would have approved, but I was very stealthy and scarfed up all the treats I could find. It was a great visit.

On the day of the signing, Sally brought wine, fruit, *cheese*, and crackers. I was not allowed to go, but I could only hope and pray that Alison would remember to bring me back a bit of *cheese*.

Guess what—my Alison did not forget! "Dea, sweet girl, would you like a piece of cheese?" she asked when she came through the door later that evening.

Was she crazy? Had she lost her mind? She knew very well the answer to that. I gobbled up that pungent piece of pleasure and smacked my lips. It was a very successful book signing, at least according to my stringent criteria of whether I got any *cheese* out of it.

She told me all about the event, and then she needed to tell the white box with the plastic cord about it, too.

"They laughed at all the right parts!" she told the box.

Once again, no one used the pages of her book for firewood, even though the days were definitely getting shorter and colder and firewood may have been on their mind.

Life with Alison was back to perfect. She threw my toys for me in the morning with a practiced arm. She hummed when she gave me my dinner and tied back my ears in a ponytail. I occasionally got a tiny piece of piquant *cheese*.

The only sour note was when she screeched in my ear again, endangering my hearing. It was when Sally got Alison a gig speaking at the JCC, which was apparently a big deal.

"You don't mean *the* JCC," she said to Sally. "The Jewish Community Center? In Manhattan?"

"I do, indeed," said Sally.

Alison gave another screech, and I really had to jump off her lap and hunt through Sally's apartment for more treats leftover by the quivering chihuahuas, who had crammed themselves behind a folded-up step stool leaning against a wall, as if I couldn't see them. They squinted their eyes shut just a little, because as everyone knows, when dogs close their eyes, no one can see them. But I am a very alert poodle, and I could see them just fine.

"It's a brunch, sweet girl," Alison told me later. "They want me to speak about having the chutzpah to move to a foreign country. But I've never done public speaking before. How am I ever going to manage?"

That was her glass-half-empty voice coming out. I recognized it by now. There was only one sure cure for that—talking nonstop to the plastic box with the cord. Alison doesn't have a green blanket to hold with her teeth, but she has that box, and when she talks to it a lot, she starts to calm down.

"But what if I don't know what to say?" she asked it. "What if the audience asks questions I can't answer?"

She went on and on, even while I dozed on her lap, but eventually, after calling the box the names of just about all her friends, her pulse returned to normal and she remembered to give me a *cookie*.

The day came for her squeal-inducing event at the JCC. She spent a long time putting on face paint and nice clothes. Oh, for those who don't know, "nice clothes" are fabrics that have a great mouth-feel but that are off limits for the likes of me. "No jumping," Alison would say. "I'm wearing nice clothes."

She was still wearing nice clothes when she got home from her event, but she swooped me up in her arms anyway and moved with me to music like she had done a long time ago. Best of all, it didn't have anything to do with a new man in her life who spelled trouble.

"They told me fifty people, and seventy-five showed up!" she said. "They had to get more chairs!"

People in the audience asked her how she managed to pick up and move to Italy when she didn't have friends there or a job lined up, and it made Alison think of all the things she had managed to accomplish in her life that didn't look like much while she was going through them, but in retrospect were quite challenging.

"Sometimes I forget all that I have done," she told me. "Maybe I do have the guts to handle life after all."

To me, handling life was a snap, as long as Alison was by my side and scratching me with just the right pressure behind one ear. But something came along to test us both.

It began when mornings, which used to be all about me and throwing my toy, were now about turning on the box with moving pictures and watching faces talk about the same thing, all the time, every day.

A virus.

Virus, this. Virus, that. Alison sat there in the morning glued to the box, hearing the word over and over, forgetting all about me even though she hugged me close, a little too tightly for my taste.

It wasn't like when she and Ted used to have a coma while they stared at the box. If anything, Alison was more alert than ever. Sometimes her body shivered, although not as much as the chihuahuas at Sally's. When she finally got out of bed, I eagerly awaited a tug-of-war with the long tail on my zebra stuffed animal, but what did she do? She went to the room with the don't-jump-on-those couches and turned on another box with pictures. She squeezed me too tightly while the faces in the box talked about the same thing. Corona, this. Corona, that. The faces looked very serious, and their voices were stern and scolding. "We still don't know what it all means," said one.

Fine, then. I suggest we move on to playing with my new zebra toy until someone figures out what it all means. But Alison threw the zebra a few times without enthusiasm. She was not moving on.

This happened over quite a few mornings, and each time I would have to nudge her with my snout to remind her that I needed to take her for her walk. On one of these mornings, we ran into Jackson, my favorite, the golden-colored Havanese who knows just how to sniff me without being offensive. "His name is Jackson, for Jackson

Heights, where we love to get momo dumplings," said Stan, one of his two humans. "Also, it's a very dignified name, and Jackson is a dignified dog."

Jackson was out walking Stan and Arthur, but the humans were acting strangely, rushing away from us without stopping for the usual chat.

"We have to shop before the shelves are empty," said Stan.

"But it's not even noon," said Alison.

"You'd be surprised. Even the big-box stores are out of toilet paper."

I guess I have to explain that people are very touchy about their toilet paper. They're obsessed with it. They walk past nice dirt patches all the time in the park, or long concrete spaces outside their buildings, and instead of doing their business and being proud of it, they wait until they have enough toilet paper and then lock themselves up in little rooms with it. Go figure.

Jackson wasn't the only dog on the block having to deal with freaked-out humans whose eyes bulged out of their heads from watching the faces in the boxes talk about "virus" and "COVID" and how they don't know anything but they insist on yapping about it anyway. People scurried away from us, and even the ones who stopped to chat with Alison while I tussled with my dog friends stood so far away, it was hard to make out what they were saying.

I was ecstatic to see Lola, with her kohl-rimmed eyes, but her person, Jessie, said something from far away that made my Alison agitated.

"Did you hear?" said Jessie—ironically from a distance of several feet away, so it was hard to hear, but the irony was lost on her. "They're closing the gym!"

"*Our* gym?" said Alison.

"Yes, the one in the building. I think the big chains are still open, if you have a membership, but I wouldn't chance it."

"Oh, no," said Alison, sounding as alarmed as the faces on the box with moving pictures. "I need my daily endorphins!"

Alison says she gets her endorphins, which I guess are energy vitamins of some kind, by running on a machine that goes nowhere and whose purpose eludes me. Right across the street from our building is a perfectly good park full of *squirrels* that need chasing.

"What will happen to your job, Jessie?" asked Alison.

"Yeah, not much going on for flautists right now," said Jessie. "They're closing down most of the city, including the New York Philharmonic. I don't know when I'll be able to work again."

At least now she won't be leaving me alone every day while she runs in place for no good reason. That's a plus. But, between Jackson's people and Lola's lady, Alison was all whipped up with a feeling of urgency that instead of going to the park, where we had been headed, she needed to go to a store full of empty shelves where she could panic some more. Sounded silly to me, but Alison had now joined the throngs of people who apparently suffered from a mass shopping delusion.

In the coming days, Alison started buying more and more of things we didn't need, stocking our home for Armageddon. If the store shelves weren't empty before, they certainly were after Alison had gotten at them. Tins of tuna and boxes of spaghetti. Canned goods with pictures of beans on the label. And, of course, toilet paper.

Our lives, which had just been starting to open up after Alison had finally stopped having first dates and after she stopped having that pain on one side, were becoming quite dreary, with the stern faces inside the picture boxes yapping about the virus. Instead of buying me more treats, Alison would come home with packages of foul-smelling hand sanitizer.

One day, she came home with a package of something that turned out to be extremely silly—a cloth that she put over her nose and all the way down to cover her mouth. If she thought my kisses were a little slobbery, she should have told me, instead of buying a slobber-kiss protector to stop me from giving her my slurpy kisses! That's just low. Plus, I now have to figure out what she is saying just by studying her eyes. This is tricky business, even for the gifted poodle I am. First, she made me learn Italian, and now I had to figure out what she meant without her face showing. I was not liking this new game.

"The city is in crisis, monkey girl," she said with her voice muffled through the antislobber cloth. "We need to be very careful. Even dogs can get this virus, so a lot of your doggie friends are leaving the city."

The news was a blow. But despite Alison's anxiety about this lockdown thing, I was having a blast.

A lockdown was when every day was a weekend day where you didn't have to go out and you could just stay home with your favorite dog, ahem, and you could take longer walks because humans complained there was nothing else to do, and that was because they hadn't looked in the toy box lately. Were they kidding? There was plenty to do!

Lockdown was also a special time when "the shelves are empty," and that was because people stocked up on everything that was important in case of an apocalypse: pancake batter, banana bread mix, *cookies*, and twirly noodles like in Italy. There was probably a law that said those were the only things you were allowed to have during a lockdown.

If there was any more room in the pantry or the entranceway where those items piled high, then it was time to redecorate by stacking family packs of bathroom tissue, especially if only one person lived in the house. Every person in the park complained they couldn't find bathroom tissue because *the shelves are empty*, but no one admitted they had already managed somehow to secretly stockpile enough to last them the rest of their lives.

There were puzzling things about the lockdown, too. We had to take a different path than our usual one in the park. There was a metal fence and a smell of dirt and dust that tickled my nose where we used to walk. The fence reminded me of my first crate as a puppy because it had closed me inside and I had been unable to get out. Now we couldn't get in.

"They're doing construction, sweet girl," Alison explained. "They're making a new play area, I think, so we'll have to walk around it."

Construction was when they tore down perfectly good things, including benches and shrubs where I and many other dogs have painstakingly applied our scent. All that work and all that good pee gone to waste. Once they finished, I would have to redouble my efforts to restore it to the nice, smelly state it was in before they ruined everything.

Construction was also when big, scary machinery either made a lot of rubble or picked up a lot of rubble. They should make up their minds! The machines clanked and beeped and made threatening noises, as if *they* were the alphas, which is laughable! Nevertheless, I stay tight with my Alison whenever they make that noise. You don't have to tell me to "heel" twice.

Once we were past the metal gates, we saw lots of new *squirrels* that I did not recognize from our usual walks. Oho, do they have a thing coming!

They did not know who they were messing with. If only Alison would let me off the leash, those *squirrels* would be toast.

Instead, I had to trade them glare for glare as they pinpointed their beady little black eyes at me while holding their nuts. Cowards!

Normally I am a poodle who likes my routine, but some of the new things we started to do during the lockdown were not as tragically bad as I first thought. Alison wanted to go on a bike path that had a lot of huff-and-puff uphill parts because the gym was closed and she needed to huff and puff every day. That's what a gym is for, by the way, to make people miserable with their huffing and puffing, but they get "addicted" and need more misery like that all the time or they get cranky. Whereas I do not huff and puff. I simply climb the hill, like any dog, but better.

"By going uphill, we're toning our legs," Alison huffed and puffed.

Thank you, but my legs were sufficiently toned. I was born that way.

We ended up in a lush area of the park with sprawling trees on both sides of the wide promenade.

"Dea, go choose a bench for us to sit on, sweet girl," said Alison. This was an awesome responsibility and I wanted to get it right, so I sniffed around for quite a while before choosing the absolute best bench. It was under a gigantic tree and had a view of the river down below. "Perfect, monkey!"

I sat on my Alison's lap facing the river as she held me tightly in her arms. "We can't touch anything. We can't go anywhere. We have to be very careful," she said, sounding a bit down.

I looked into her eyes because that was all I could see, thanks to the antikissing cloth covering her face, and placed my paw on her arm. I saw I would have to help her through this lockdown.

After our bench sit, we walked down a winding path all the way toward the river and home.

We had plenty of bottles of water and family packs of bathroom tissue, but there were no people. They seemed to have vanished. "There's no one left on our floor except us!" said Alison. Except for the sound the elevator machine made in the hallway after Alison pressed a button, there was a ghostly silence. Even my politest of barks echoed down the long corridor in a spooky way, as if there were ghostly dogs barking, too. I was aware of the sound of my toenails scrabbling on the floor.

On days when it rained, we couldn't go out, because people melt if they get wet. I'm an all-weather type of dog, but humans are very delicate and cannot get wet except in their bathrooms. They are afraid of rain and drizzle and have to put on plastic hats and hold things over their heads. When it rained during the lockdown, Alison played fast music very loud and danced around so she could huff and puff indoors.

"Back in the day, they called me a disco queen!" she said between huffs and puffs as she twirled crazily and flung her arms out. Then she raised her arms up and down and side to side until I thought maybe she needed a v-e-t to help her calm down.

"I've got endorphins, baby!" she said.

Endorphins are things you get when you huff and puff a lot, and once you have them you think you own the world and you make lots of plans in your head for the amazing things you will do with your amazing powers, and then when you sit down for a little while, the endorphins go somewhere else and you remember that you do not own the world and therefore do not have to do any of those amazing things after all, which will free up a lot of time for staring at the moving pictures on the box that everyone has in their bedroom.

Alison listened to Quincy Jones and the Trammps, calling out the names of the songs and the singers as she continued to stamp around and summon endorphins from who knows where. I was scared at first, especially because she stepped on a few of my finer squeaky toys, including the red lobster. I thought it best to hide beneath the couch and watch this madness from a safe distance.

After about a hundred songs by the Bee Gees, Alison finally plopped down on a mat that she rolled out onto the floor. She stretched the way I do after I wake up from a long nap.

It seemed safe to approach her now that the endorphins had packed up and left, so I went over and gave her ear kisses, which made her laugh. Then I pulled her long hair, which did not make her laugh, but I couldn't help it if she didn't have as finely tuned a sense of humor as I did.

She was still doing stretches on the floor when she flicked on the moving-picture box in the living room. The small people inside the box were yapping some more about the virus. They sounded very serious. Alison stopped stretching and her face went stiff. Her endorphins were really gone now, and she was remembering she did not rule the world after all and that the world was a scary, uncertain place.

Our bedroom door had always been closed when we went to sleep, but after that night, she kept the door propped open just enough for me to get out and into the wee-wee-pad room that had my water bowl.

"They hardly know anything about this virus," she said. "If I should get it . . ."

Her voice trailed off. She got up and packed a little bag with my toys and instructions, the way she usually did when I went to babysit Sue. She put it by the big door to the hallway.

"Just in case," she said, "because I always need to know you will be all right."

Lockdown

Alison and I were together nearly all the time now. Even if she went out to look at the empty store shelves with the antisloppy-kiss shield covering her face, she was back before I woke from my nap and while I was still clutching my green blanket.

Then the world turned bitter and gray one day when I heard her talking to the plastic box with the cord. There was a little man inside the box whose voice I did not recognize.

"You say you're a psychiatrist?" she said.

"My own practice," said the tiny man.

"I have a master's in social work. Looks like we might have things in common."

My Alison was at it again. Even though there was a lockdown, she was back to that "online" place where the men are too warm sometimes to wear shirts. I thought we had finished with this terrible phase she was going through, but no.

"Been on this site long?" the little man asked her.

"I haven't been on in ages, but with the lockdown, there's really no other way to meet anyone," said Alison.

"I agree. Everything is so isolating these days."

I made a doggie groan and squeaked my alligator toy to show my displeasure. To me, this new man spelled trouble.

"He sounded so normal," Alison told me later. "He said he'd like to check in with me every Sunday so we have a little routine. Hey, this is giving me energy!"

To my horror, she blasted more Bee Gees music and started leaping about and throwing her arms here and there.

Suddenly, she dropped to the floor and made a terrible sound.

"*Ow!*" she screeched.

I raced right over to help her with my healing kisses, but they didn't seem to work.

"My back," she groaned. "I must've pulled something."

She dragged herself into our bedroom and lay on our bed, where I continued to give her doggie CPR consisting of copious applications of doggie saliva.

I knew she needed a v-e-t, and I also somehow knew she wouldn't go see one. "Nothing's open," she said, "and the places that are open are full of people with the virus.

Eventually, though, even she had to admit she needed help. She stretched some thin, plastic-looking gloves over her hands and put an antislobber shield over her face. She left me alone with sirens and noises outside. I dashed to get my green blanket and beat on the door with my paws, but it was no use.

My Alison was gone.

She never returned. Well, she did return, but it felt like never. She said she had been to an urgent care facility.

"Dea, it was awful. When I got there, everyone was coughing. It was like I could see a fog of germs all around them. I had to wait outside and have them text me when the doctor could see me, like those restaurants where they give you something to hold that vibrates when your table is ready."

This was a little confusing, but apparently the v-e-t finally had a table ready for Alison, and he had her lie on top of it so he could move her body around.

"He said I pulled a few muscles in my lower back and I'll need to rest and take a pill," she said. "Don't you worry, monkey. By tomorrow I'll be good as new."

I took exception to that, because although Alison is always splendid in my eyes, she was not as good as new. I took her for her full walk, but we did not go on the huff-and-puff bike path uphill. She was already huffy and puffy just from walking on flat ground. We had to sit on several benches for a rest, not just the perfect one I chose for us.

What was worse, she cut the walk short for a very terrible reason: The little man in the plastic box was due to call at five o'clock, and we had to get back on time.

Although Alison's back got better over time, and we again took the huffy-puffy bike path, our Sunday walks always had to be hurried and frantic because we had to get home in time for the little man in the plastic box. She said we had a "schedule" to keep. Well, the only schedule I thought we should keep was the one I liked to follow, which involved Alison throwing my favorite toy in the morning, Alison tying my ears back in a ponytail and putting out breakfast, and all the other things that were urgent and necessary in the course of my day. Nowhere in this agenda was a little man in a stupid little box.

"But isn't this great?" she said. "He always does what he says, and always on time!"

I could not share her enthusiasm. These shenanigans had already gone on for several months.

"He's so reliable! He likes to travel! He loves Italian food!" burbled Alison.

Sorry, not impressed. I, too, was reliable. I had traveled extensively in cars where I upchucked on occasion, but in a very polite way. And I loved twisty noodles with *cheese*. I did not see what was so special about the little man in the plastic box.

On our walks, the restaurants started putting huts outside with tables and big, flapping pieces of plastic between them. Alison got very excited when she saw these little lean-tos with tables and plastic because she had a keen eye for architecture, I guess. "Soon we'll be able to eat at restaurants again!" she said.

Just when I, too, started salivating at the thought of dining al fresco, tragedy struck.

First, a word about dining al fresco: It means eating on the sidewalk, where instead of menus, they give you a secret code, and you take out your little metal-and-glass rectangle from your bag and point it at the code, and then if you are over a certain age, like my Alison, you squint at the metal box and try to read what you are allowed to eat, and when you can't really make out what it says there, you make the waiter stand there and recite a long list of foods, and then you order the same thing you order all the time anyway.

The new tragedy was that Alison was having another first date. She was going to meet the tiny man in the box in person at one of these outdoor lean-tos, and she was going to squint at the rectangle and make the waiter recite the menu and order the same thing again, only all this would take place without *me* and with no more thought about *me* than if I were a random speck in the universe.

First, though, Alison had to decide what to wear.

"Ooh, it's been so long, I wonder if anything still fits," Alison worried, but I had walked her so many times during the lockdown, with so much huffing and puffing, that her clothing fit just fine.

That was not good enough for her, though, because the rules of first dates meant you were not allowed to wear the first thing you put on. Alison put on something bright red and silky that showed her legs—all sleek from the huffing and puffing—and she looked beautiful and glowing, but rules are rules, and she had to tear that off and try on a new outfit. The right thing to wear on a first date is the one outfit that's left after the rest of your entire wardrobe has been discarded, one by one, and piled high on the bed. Before the piling, you have to squint at yourself in a mirror and do facial exercises by scrunching your face and twisting your mouth to the side, sometimes looking angry or disgusted. This is accompanied by phrases like, "What was I thinking?" Then you take off the clothing, heap it on the bed, go back into the closet, and jangle the hangers around until you find something else. It's a long process, but I am a patient poodle, and I watched the whole thing with fascination for the strange ways of humans. They are endlessly entertaining!

Finally, Alison's bed was piled high, and she had settled on something emerald green and satiny. Best of all, she put great-smelling rawhide boats on her feet that had sticks on the bottom. They clicked and clacked on the floor when she walked the way my toenails do.

After all those angry-looking facial exercises, she was relaxed and happy. She whirled around the room. She lifted me up and held me tightly, and then she said those evil words: "I'll be back in a few hours. Be a good girl."

"Be a good girl" means "I'm abandoning you to a sad fate, but don't make a fuss about it, because you have no choice while I have a date with a man who spells trouble."

Oh, he spelled trouble, all right. Although he had called on time every Sunday for months, he showed up half an hour late for dinner in the sidewalk lean-to. Alison waited at her table, one that was as far away from the others as possible. She spent the thirty minutes waiting for Sam by fidgeting with her kiss protection and trying to keep it from smudging her lipstick.

"There you are," she said when Sam arrived. He was taller than someone who would fit inside a plastic box but a lot shorter and stouter than in his photos. Alison was accustomed to this by now because the men "online" only posted photos of themselves with special cameras that distorted all their features until they looked like *GQ* models. You had to admire technology.

"Sorry, had to wait for a parking spot to open up," said Sam. "Didn't want to pay to put my car in a garage." He was holding his kiss guard, the straps dangling from his wrist.

"You don't wear your mask?" asked Alison. She immediately realized it was not the best way to start their first in-person conversation, but she believed lockdown made people "rusty," that they were rusted so badly they forgot how to be with other people.

"Not unless it's mandatory," he said. "Would you like a glass of wine? I'm getting a pinot noir."

"Oh, that's my favorite too!" said Alison, grasping onto anything they might have in common.

"And please order whatever you like, dinner is on me."

It turned out Sam was lockdown rusty, just like Alison. Their conversation was awkward and stilted.

"So, you're divorced," said Alison. "Me too."

"My wife cheated on me."

"Sorry. It must have been tough to trust again."

"Who's the doctor now?"

Alison could have kicked herself with her stick-and-rawhide shoes. Divorce was never a fun thing to talk about, even if the rules for first dates demanded that you tick it off the topic list.

"You had a great skiing photo on your profile," Alison tried again. "You must be very good."

"Been skiing my whole life. I go so fast, it's almost like racing."

"I'm more the slower-paced gal, just taking it all in," said Alison. "It's really kind of meditative, don't you think?"

"I don't know about that. Last time I went, I broke my arm. I could hear the crunch." He cracked a breadstick in half to demonstrate.

Alison took a deep sip of her wine.

She inquired as to his work. That was always safe, since people like to yap about what they do. He finally asked about her.

"I've written my first book. It's a memoir," said Alison.

The psychiatrist sat there without saying a word. After an awkward silence, he said, "May I ask what makes your story different from any other memoir on the shelf?"

He could ask, but she didn't want to answer. It was the kind of question she didn't mind from an agent or publisher, because they have to vet new books, but when Sam asked it, she felt he was really asking whether she was worthy, and she didn't feel like having to explain or justify herself. Moving alone to Rome without speaking the language, knowing anyone, or having any work took some guts. Did Sam have guts?

"Are you making a lot of money on it?" asked Sam. "How are book sales?"

Alison coughed. The social rustiness must have spread to her throat, where it was clogging up any ability to answer appropriately, so she took a big sip of water.

It turned out she was also rusty at wearing rawhide boats with long sticks on her feet. By the time she came home to me, she had blisters.

"Oh, monkey, I give up. It was a bust," she said.

I was a little rusty at being left alone after all this together time during lockdown. Alison soon found that I had missed the wee-wee pad by an inch. She became very animated over this, talking about possible punishments and saying things like, "You should know better," but the end result was just what I wanted: Alison paid much more attention to me, at least for the moment.

"I am so disappointed in you, Dea. Bad dog," she said. But her eyes were directly on me as she said it, totally involved with me, super focused on me. It was intoxicating.

"Now go inside your crate!"

Uh-oh. This was not where I expected things to head. My tail pointed straight down like an upside-down arrow and my head hung low. I didn't move. Maybe this phase of Alison's would pass.

"I said go inside your crate!"

I didn't see the upside of going inside my crate. Alison didn't seem in the mood to give me a *cookie*, so what would I gain from doing as she said?

Alison took matters into her own hands, literally. She picked me up and plopped me inside the crate and closed the door. She hadn't done that since I was a naughty puppy and didn't know the difference between good-dog behavior and bad-dog behavior. I certainly knew the difference now, and like any great artiste, I knew the rules well enough to break them every now and then.

Anyway, I knew she could not stay angry with me long. Have you looked into my dreamy, deep-chocolate eyes lately? She was well under my spell, as any decent human would be.

She gave a loud huff and came over to open the crate door. But as she undid the lock, she lost her balance and fell backward, landing hard on the wood floor onto her right thumb, stretching it all out in the wrong direction, and howling like a wild wolf in the moonlight. "*Ow! Ow!*" she screamed.

I learned from that incident that I must never disobey her again with the wee-wee pad, ever, or soon all her fingers would be splayed in the wrong directions. And, much as I am distantly related to wolves, I did not really get along with that part of the clan and did not want to be so near one of their kind.

The next day she went back to the v-e-t, where I hoped they stamped one of those ten-for-one-free cards like they used to give out at the coffee shop for repeat visitors. She came home with a huge white bandage bulb on her right thumb, where it was painful and puffy. At least she was a lefty like me. The first time she taught me to give a handshake, I lifted my left paw, so again we have so much in common, except that I do not wear a large bandage bulb on my right paw.

Once she was home, Alison removed the bandage bulb. Underneath was a metal stick with bandage wrap that kept her thumb straight.

"They say it might be a torn ligament, but it can heal on its own," she told the plastic box with the cord. I'm glad the plastic box worries about her, but it can't worry about her as much as I do. Alison knew that, and that's why she removed the curse she had put on me earlier: "You are such a *good* girl," she said. "A *good* girl." I was glad she had corrected the record.

"I think it was karma that I got hurt by putting you in the crate," she said. "I'll never do it again, unless you don't use the wee-wee pad properly. But, I know, we're all rusty because of the lockdown."

Alison decided to correct her rustiness in the worst way possible—by going back "online" to the hot zone where the men sometimes take off their shirts. She would scope out a new guy and then press the magic button on the plastic box with the cord, and the new little man inside the box would say things like, "You're very attractive!" and "You sound so interesting!" It was getting too crowded inside that box.

The tiny new man told Alison he would drive into the city to take her to dinner. "I just live twenty minutes away."

"Sounds like a plan," she said. A plan for disaster, in my book. "I just need to check—you're being careful regarding the virus, right?"

"I don't have to be. I've already had it," he said. "Now I have all these beautiful antibodies and I'm safe. I can't get it again."

"I'm not really sure they've ascertained that," said Alison.

"Really, no need to worry. I have the beautiful antibodies."

"Yes, that's great, I'm sure they're very beautiful, but the scientists say we need to wear masks and do social distancing."

"I don't trust the science and I don't trust that Fauci guy," he said. "Hey, could you send me another photo of yourself? Make it full body."

"I'm quite fit, if that's what you're asking."

"I met a stunner last week, but she never gave me a full-length photo, and when I met her in person, her body type just wasn't right for me. It's nothing personal. Just a matter of taste."

"You know what? I don't think this is going to work," said Alison. "Best of luck with your beautiful antibodies."

She seemed mad at the little man in the little box, so I got my blue dinosaur and placed it thoughtfully in her lap. That did the trick. She threw it, I fetched it, she threw it, I fetched it. I think you get the idea.

The afternoon passed blissfully.

One of the problems with humans, though, is they have very poor short-term memory. Just as I was settling down to collect more marvelous rust from being alone with my Alison, she was back on the plastic box with the cord talking to more men from the hot zone. At least she had given up on trying to meet them in person at the lean-tos. "I'll just get to know them by phone, and when all this is over, I'll already know which ones could be keepers," she told me.

"What made you choose being an endodontist?" she asked the box while I sat on her lap, trying with my snout to divert her attention back to me. She pressed the magic button so she had her hands free to pet me in the ways to which I am entitled.

"I get paid well," said the little man with a chuckle. "Also, I truly enjoy helping people in pain." Oh, really? I am in pain just listening to this. "Do you want to meet for a drink? I'll come into the city. If we get along really well, we can enjoy a good-night kiss."

Alison's face made a crinkly shape. She took a deep breath and petted me behind my ear. "Since we're all wearing masks, I guess on the forehead is okay," she said.

"No, I mean a real kiss. No masks. Just two people with a lot in common, being together the way people were meant to be. Just two people . . ."

"I have something on the stove," said Alison, and that was the end of the little endodontist in the little box.

She buried her face in my lovely hair and sighed. "Dea, it's not any better talking to these guys now than it was before this health crisis," she said. "They're all nuts. I'm through with them."

That's the ticket! She went to fetch my leash so I could take her for a walk, and that's when I heard that awful ding sound coming from the little metal-and-glass rectangle that every human carries and often stares at in a coma. She grabbed it and read things from the screen with great interest and an occasional chuckle. "Oh, this one says he's a traveling nurse!"

Hey, what happened to "they're all nuts?"

I didn't know why "traveling nurse" sounded so appealing to her. We don't want anyone wandering around here, now or ever. If they needed to travel, they should travel out the big door and go to far-off places and never come back, like the Italian guy who was so scared of my Alison he had to travel the ocean and cower on the other side.

"He says he works at a hospital in the city and lives about an hour away," she told me. "He didn't exactly answer about where he lives, but I'll ask him again."

She typed out her question, and this time he came back with the information that he lived in a big house without a lease, paying one month at a time and sharing with three other people.

"He doesn't sound too settled," said Alison, chewing on the one thumb that was not in a metal splint.

The metal rectangle dinged again, and she peered at the screen. "He's saying I won't be disappointed," she told me. "I wonder what, exactly, he means?"

What he means, I think, is that he spells trouble.

I finally took Alison for her walk, but I hadn't seen a lot of my canine friends in an eternity. Where did they go?

"Everyone's gone to stay at their weekend houses until this whole thing passes over," said Alison.

A weekend house is a place that's "more trouble than it's worth," but the people who had one were happy they did during the lockdown because it allowed them to "commune with nature" and have the wonderful opportunity to pay for two places at one time, without living at all in one of them.

The only dog left seemed to be Boris, the nasty white German shepherd who wears a muzzle and once knocked over his human while he was standing on his two hind legs to growl at me like a grizzly bear. We avoided him and went deeper into the park, avoiding the metal fence where they were doing noisy, cough-inducing construction. I carefully chose the perfect bench we would sit on for the day when a super-friendly goldendoodle lunged at me to give me a sloppy kiss even before a sniff. He brought his person, a friendly young woman, over with him.

"This is Ozzie," said the woman. "Do you mind if we sit here with you? Ozzie has no one to play with these days."

"This is Dea, which means goddess in Italian," said Alison, as she always explains about me. "Oh, and I'm Alison."

"I'm Rosie," said the woman, laughing. "It's all about the dogs, isn't it?" They laughed their fool heads off.

"I named him Ozzie because he's like the Wizard of Oz. He has real magical powers," said Rosie.

"I'll bet he does!" said Alison, although why she should lie like that is beyond me. She knows very well that the only thing with true magical powers is my green blanket.

Rosie petted me perfectly under my chin and Alison stroked Ozzie all over his back because it's true what she said. It's all about the dogs.

The humans agreed to meet for lunch sometime, and Ozzie and I played and played like we had never played before. I didn't know about the humans, but Ozzie and I were not the least bit rusty. Then we all sat together on the bench and watched the sun change color.

A Boatload of Fun

There was something wrong with Alison's hair. She often looked at it in the mirror and moaned. I pulled it whenever I could, to get it back to the way she liked it, but nothing was working.

"It's too long," she said. "When will the salons open again, monkey girl?"

I didn't have the answer to that. I don't know why humans are so obsessed with their hair salons. No one likes a shampoo, I can tell you from personal experience.

"But guess what, monkey girl? You are the lucky one, because the salons for dogs are open! It's time for your shampoo and cut."

This did not make me the lucky one, no siree. The only good thing about a trip to the groomer was that I got to trot out my exceptional dramatic skills. Whenever Alison was about to leave me at one of these torture dungeons, I would look at her like she was abandoning me to the depths of Hades. My body trembled like a chihuahua, and I turned my chocolate eyes into giant saucers of fear.

"I don't think I can leave her like this," said Alison to the evil shampoo lady.

"Don't worry, the minute you leave she's totally fine," the shampoo demon lied.

Once I was alone with the shampoo sorceress, it was time for the torture. She placed me in a big, hard container with water and rubbed a rancid-smelling perfumed cream all over me. She rubbed it into my hair, which would make the smell hard for me to get out—I would have to find a nice mud puddle very soon and do my poodle best—and then kept pouring more water all over me until I was quite bedraggled. I shook my body from front to middle to back, fiercely, spraying water all over the shampoo girl and her floor, which I am positive she enjoyed. Then she used a hot machine on me that made a scary noise while she exclaimed over and over that I was the most beautiful dog in the world—which, although true, was simply a ruse to make me cooperate.

Was the torture over? It was not. Once I had no water left to shake off, she cut my beautiful, curly black poodle hair. Just chopped it off. No respect.

I felt a little better about the whole sordid affair when Alison returned and exclaimed, "Dea, you look gorgeous!" She held me up to a long piece of glass to show me a different dog that looked something like me, and then dispensed with that silliness by hugging me tightly and sniffing my hair. Don't worry, mama, I'll get rid of that awful perfume smell as soon as we see the next mud puddle.

Now that my Alison was mine again and telling me how lovely, special, and spectacular I was, I pranced out of the store with my head held high like I should have been wearing a tiara and a strand of pearls. Which was not a bad idea, come to think of it.

We continued our lockdown routine of starting each day with long, huffy-puffy walks. Alison only left me if she had to go buy food from the empty shelves. I continued honing my theatrical skills by working on my moaning cries and door beating, even though Alison didn't really stay out very long, I had to admit, since there was not very much to buy from the empty shelves.

"Dea, we need a break," said Alison.

I perked up my ears—first one, then the other. I must remind you that a break is a time-out before you explode, but there was nothing to explode about. Life with Alison was perfect. I had her just where I wanted her.

"Let's go back to that place in Connecticut for a redo," she said. "I feel too isolated here."

Isolated? I beg your humble pardon. She had me all day and all night, so in what way was she isolated?

"I need some human company, sweet girl," she said.

I was about to harrumph, but I knew it was true. I didn't know what I would do without Iggy. Everyone needs somebody to sniff every now and again.

We returned to the hotel in Connecticut, where Steffi, the manager, greeted us like long-lost family. Even though she and Alison both wore their antis-loppy-kiss shields, at least now Alison had someone to sniff and everything would be okay.

In our room, my paws slipped around on the smooth floor until I could stop myself on the area rug. There was a soft, cushiony covering on the bed that I jumped onto and rolled around on.

Then, I smelled something quite new and exciting.

"Look what Steffi gave you, sweet girl," said Alison.

It was brand-new yellow giraffe squeaky toy with a super long neck, perfect for chewing. I tried it out and I can report it had an excellent squeaky sound. The way to know whether a new toy has a good sound is when your human hears it for the first time and screws up her face. I believe that is a sign of serene pleasure and musical appreciation. If you do not achieve the desired effect from your human at first, just keep trying. Eventually they will come around and screw up their face.

Alison received a present from Steffi, too, but it was not nearly as exciting as mine. It was a box of chocolates that did not squeak in the least; plus, "Dogs can't eat chocolate." It's another one of those human laws, so I've never tried any, but chocolate doesn't squeak or crunch, and you can't throw it and fetch it, so what really is the purpose? Alison didn't act disappointed, but she is very polite that way.

Steffi also left a card. "She wants us to come with her on a boat tomorrow," said Alison. "You won't need your pink life vest—it's totally safe—and none of that nasty waterskiing, either! There will be other people to talk to."

I was happy to hear my mariner skills would not go to waste, although I did miss the pink life vest. I looked very fetching in it. If only Alison would get one of her own and we could go out to restaurants in our matching outfits. I think everyone would stare at us with great appreciation for our fashionista ways!

We went outdoors onto a terrace where we could sit and watch the huge boats bobbing on the gray-blue water. One was so long and tall that I longed to jump aboard and run up and down the deck and play pirate. I hoped that was the boat we would be on the next day when Steffi took us on a tour of Long Island Sound.

We took our old walk around the water, and again I smelled the most deliciously fishy scents. Sublimely pungent. Our "break" was going very well so far, with no one exploding. I remembered the roasted chicken Alison had left behind beneath the metal dome last time we were here, and I wondered if it was still here somewhere. I sniffed all over, looking for it, because that, too, had a delicious aroma that I longed to experience again.

When we returned to the hotel, Steffi was there at the entrance. Since she was the manager, I believe she was required to stand there at the entrance all day and all night to greet dogs and their people. That's why she gets the big bucks—which is a phrase Alison has used in the past and said was really some kind of a joke. Although if it's a joke, I don't get it. People with very busy jobs and no time to themselves are the ones who get the big bucks, but I don't know where they keep their herd of deer. Do they also run zoos?

I jumped up on Steffi's legs to give her knee a hug because her face was unavailable. She had on her unkissable covering. I could smell her *cat*, which was unfortunate. I wondered if her cat knew Precious; probably so, because all cats know all other cats and meet for secret witchy cabals to scheme about ways to take over the world and eject dogs. Normally, I am an easygoing poodle, but cats make me a little nervous because I don't know what they're thinking or why they have to sit in a lump like a meatloaf sometimes.

I had become quite good during the lockdown at recognizing people from their eye expressions. It takes a real talent to do that, but talent is what I have in abundance. I could tell if they were smiling or angry, just by their eyes. It really wasn't that hard. I did the same sort of thing with dogs, because sometimes a new dog's tail didn't wag and I needed to look into their eyes to get a feel for their temperament before I sniffed. You can't be too careful.

"No trips to the ER so far?" Steffi asked. Her eyes were smiling, so I knew she was joking.

"Not yet, knock wood," said Alison. She looked around and found the back of a chair to knock on. Oh, these humans are a laugh riot with their funny ways!

We both slept well that night. Alison put those little plugs into her ears, but there were no bigwigs outside our room making noise this time. The mean man from last time, the one that acted like a German shepherd, must have shipped out to sea on his yacht.

The next day we had our walk near the fishy smells, although I also had to watch Alison run, run, run to nowhere on a machine inside the hotel gym. Very dull. I slept through most of it.

Later, when there was a nice afternoon lull, we met Steffi in the lobby where she obviously lived full time so she could collect the big bucks and put them in a zoo. She took us for our fabulous sea adventure.

"The hotel has a little boat we use for special guests," said Steffi as she led us along a wooden plank near a line of bobbing boats. I was happy to hear we were her special guests, and I looked at Alison to see if she needed to knock wood again. There was plenty of it all around on the walkway, but she seemed fine at the moment.

The hotel boat was not the giant pirate ship I had scoped out, unfortunately, but it was still a perfectly good craft for a special guest like *moi*. There were multiple places to sit, and even one beneath a covering so we could get out of the hot sun. There was a man with strange markings all over his arms and neck who smelled smoky and said he would drive the boat and take us far enough out so we could see the ocean.

I sat on my Alison's lap facing forward as a loud roar started and the boat began hurtling out into the open water. This was exhilarating! The wind wafted lots of salty, fishy scents right up my nose and blew my long, silky black ears back, where they flapped in the breeze. I didn't know where to look first! There were so many big boats just sitting on top of the water, and in one direction there was a lot of land and in another direction very big houses that had little boats of their own tied to places where you could knock on wood all day and never run out of the stuff.

The man with the arm and neck markings who drove the boat knew who owned what, and he called out their names as we passed their big boats and bigger houses. "Super rich," he yelled over the roar about one. "Very wealthy and has two yachts," he yelled about another. This man knew just about everything in the world. I wanted Alison to have a first date with him, but later she told me she didn't care for tattoos. I don't know why that would be an issue, because the body markings were probably just notes to himself to remember who owned what. You can't walk around with all that information stuffed in your brain and not have a few pieces of it fall out.

The best part of the adventure was the salty, smelly water splashing right in my face and making a fantastically messy puddle in the bottom of the boat. This was the way life should be. I wanted this every day.

Alison and Steffi were yap, yap, yapping the whole way about their lives, totally missing out on how wonderful it was to have sea spray in their faces and puddles on the floor. This was why humans needed help meditating, because they could not see the wonders that were right in front of them.

Our ocean adventure lasted only two seconds, or that's how it felt. I made a little fuss about leaving it all behind, because I wanted more of it, but I didn't want to ruin my "good girl" streak and there were still a few pleasures in store.

We had two fun meals out before we finished taking our break. The first was with Alison's friends in Connecticut, Amy and Ben. They wore unkissable face masks, but I gave them knee hugs. When I jumped into Ben's lap, he stroked my back nonstop. He had a comfy lap and a big, soft belly. It was so nice that when Alison took me back, I whimpered, and Ben said it was okay, I could stay with him, so they passed me over the table like a football and I got to stay nestled against his big soft belly. I hope Alison gets a big, soft belly like that. Wouldn't that be super? She would have to stop going to the gym, though, and quit all the huffing and puffing. Then she would have to eat an awful lot of black-and-white *cookies* to get the kind of plush softness that Ben had. It could take months. But I would try to urge her to stop moving and start expanding. It was for my comfort, after all.

The next night, we had dinner with Steffi in a dark restaurant with a slippery floor. Other dogs had to wait outside, but they let me in because word had gotten around about how extremely well behaved I was at the table. I was so proud of my accomplishments that I sort of forgot the good behavior part, and I put my paws on the table and sniffed everyone's plates.

"Dea, what's come over you?" said Alison.

"It's okay, she's not hurting anyone," said Steffi, who still smelled of *cat* but seemed like a nice person otherwise.

It was the last night of our break, and I was hoping someone would remember to locate the roasted chicken Alison had left behind beneath the metal dome, but apparently no one could locate it. Everyone ordered something fishy at the dark restaurant. I still missed that chicken, and I probably will for the rest of my life.

Back at the hotel, a big, hulking bulldog named Hercules, with a jutting-out tooth, came rushing over to greet me. He must have heard about me and wanted to bask in my stardom. He sniffed me with a passion I had never experienced.

"Hello, little man. It seems you're not fixed," said Alison, moving him away from me.

I shuddered involuntarily when I heard the word "fixed." I have a long-ago memory of what that meant—having to wear a plastic cone over my head so I couldn't scratch, scratch, scratch the itch, itch, itch that the v-e-t had given me.

That night, I played with my new toy from Steffi until I fell asleep on the plush bed covering. We had had the most sublime break, with no trips on rolling beds to the v-e-t and no German-shepherd men yelling in the hallways.

Once we were back home, Alison ran out to the empty shelves to buy milk and said she would be right back. I curled up in front of the big door contentedly. I didn't even need my green blanket.

The Gate Comes Down

There came a time when I had to babysit Sue again, "just for the day," because Alison needed to go to the V-E-T for a checkup at the place where she did *not* have a PET scan—and because Sue was still just as hopeless as ever and needed supervision. She had a whole new crew of dogs walking her along with me; we pulled as a team, in different directions of course. Later, each member of the dog team went to their homes, and I came back with Sue to her place, where the dreadful Precious gave me the evil eye and immediately lay down on my blue doughnut so that there was no room for me. I tried to get in there next to her, but she started making little open-shut movements with her paws against my hair and she made that motor sound deep in her chest.

"Oh, look, she's making biscuits!" said Sue, as if that were a good thing.

You know how some people look at their pets and instead of a normal look coming out of their eyes, it's all twinkles and fairy dust? That's Sue looking at Precious, in a nutshell.

I really needed my beauty nap, so I gradually wedged myself into the doughnut along with Precious. We were all up against each other, kind of cuddled, but what could I do? I simply could not dislodge the baleful creature.

I grew accustomed to the motor sound in her chest after a while and began to doze off. Her biscuit-making on my hair was like a massage.

In no time, I started dreaming of the *squirrel*. There he was, the horrible thing, squinting his beady eyes at me and chittering like he was trying to tell me something.

"Come closer," he said.

I knew it was a trick, but I was curious.

"Closer," he said.

I was at the foot of the tree, looking up at him on a high branch.

"I have a secret to tell you," he chittered.

"What secret? Tell it to me now!"

The *squirrel* looked around to make sure no one was listening, and he told me his secret in a voice so soft I really had to listen hard to make it out above the far-off purring of Precious.

"I'm your friend," said the *squirrel*.

Oh, I am not falling for that one! I harrumphed in my sleep and found a new position that unfortunately got me even more intertwined with the awful Precious. Then I fell into a dreamless, blissful sleep.

When I woke up, I was a bit dazed. It took me a while to remember I was babysitting Sue and that I had dreamed the *squirrel* liked me. I immediately became oriented to my surroundings when I saw Precious sitting in a meatloaf position and staring at me with evil intent.

I wondered whether the *squirrel* had some wisdom after all in its *squirrelly* little way. I thought I would try it out.

"I have a secret," I sent in ESP thought waves to Precious.

"Who cares?" she sent back via animal ESP.

"I'm your friend," I sent to her, undaunted.

She took a little swat at me. Still, I knew we'd be sharing my blue doughnut again at some point, because there was no way I could leave the hopeless Sue on her own forever.

Alison returned just in time for me to walk her. She was in a buoyant mood. "They gave me an all-clear, at least for now, sweet girl," she said.

"We can't know the future, but at least we have right now."

We pranced together into the park, happy as could be, and there we saw something truly amazing—they had finally taken down the metal fence! The big, noisy equipment was gone, the dust had stopped tickling my nose, and a new part of the park was ready for us to explore.

We saw a large promenade with a smooth new pavement that didn't make me trip. There were tables and benches for picnics. "Dea, look, we can eat outside," said Alison.

I smelled sweet-smelling new things hanging from bushes. Some were purple and some were as pink as my life jacket.

"They've made a refuge," said Alison. "Isn't it pretty?"

Pretty smelly, she meant, and that was a good thing.

There were so many new wooden benches where I could choose the perfect one for sitting and Alison could knock wood, if ever she needed to. Many of these benches faced the river, perfect for when I wanted to see ducks waddle in a way that invited me to pounce on them, if only Alison would let me off the leash and if only I had a killer instinct, like cats, which are little murder machines with soft fur.

Or were the ducks my friends, too? I was still mighty conflicted about that dream I'd had.

We ran into Reggie, my golden retriever pal, and when I say "ran into," I mean he actually tackled me, on purpose so that our leashes would tangle. I knew my Alison and Reggie's Nellie really enjoyed having to untangle them. It obviously gave them great pleasure and a chance to repeat our names over and over in a state of great excitement. "Dea!" "Reggie!" They just kept repeating our names, and a fun time was had by all.

Then I saw him. The white Maltese who had such a crush on me that sometimes Alison had to pull him away from me "because we live in a civilized world," she said.

We hadn't seen Herbie and his human, Bruna, since near the start of the lockdown. "Bruna, it's been forever!" said Alison.

"We've been at the summer house, but we missed the city," said Bruna. "And I see Herbie missed Dea."

"Dea!" shouted Alison. She pulled me away slightly before he started to get extra intimate with his sniffing and attempts to hump. It was okay. Humping was just his thing.

"Herbie!" shouted Bruna.

It was just like old times.

"How did you stay busy out at the house?" asked Alison.

"I've taken up a new hobby, and I'm really into it. Zucchini."

"The vegetable? That's a hobby?"

"You'd be surprised! When there's nothing else to do, you can get really into gardening, and it turns out I have a green thumb for zucchini. Not so much for tomatoes, but when you need a good zucchini, you come to me."

Alison laughed, which was a good sound to hear. "I'll keep that in mind," she said. "Do you think all the regulars are starting to come back? It's been so lonely."

"I saw Ellen and Cody just the other day," said Bruna. "They have a different walking schedule now that Ellen is working from home instead of the office, but I'm sure you'll run into them."

"Dea would love to see Lola. That's her best friend."

"Is that the one who looks like she's wearing eyeliner? Jessie's Lola?" They both laughed. "She's like the Marilyn Monroe of dogs."

I stopped playing with Herbie just long enough to give Bruna a little snort. Marilyn Monroe is the Lola of humans. She ought to know better.

When it was time to move along, I gave Bruna a knee hug since she, too, was wearing an antisloppy-kiss shield on her face, and everyone deserves a hug and a slurpy kiss from a dog, no matter where on the body it lands.

"She's doing her koala bear thing," Alison said to Bruna, because when I rise up on my hind legs to my full height and wrap my front paws around a person's knees, I don't let go.

As we explored the new area of the park that had been gated off for so long, we saw that we were not alone. There were lots of dogs with their people. The world was feeling full again. And my paws were feeling . . . sensational! What was that silky, smooth stuff they had put on the ground?

"That's sand, monkey. They made a little beach, like the one you played on when you were just a puppy."

We tried out the new paths. We didn't have to take the old one with forty-nine steps anymore if we didn't feel like it. There were winding paths and straight paths.

Along came a white Boston terrier who was so tiny I couldn't believe it. "He's a pandemic puppy, just four months old," explained his human. "He's Winston. I'm Marcus."

"This is Dea. It means goddess in Italian, and her middle name is Della Vita, so her full name means goddess of life." Oh, no, Alison is ruining the moment by giving the full history of my name again! When will she stop embarrassing me?

But she was in good company, because Marcus began doing the same thing. "Mine's Winston, after Winston Churchill, because he's a real leader. He controls our household, anyway."

Alison and Marcus laughed their fool heads off. Humans like to explain their dogs' names over and over and then laugh and laugh. It's not just because they're rusty from the lockdown. They were always this way. I think it's important to them to embarrass their dogs, or maybe to pretend to each other that because they dole out the names, they are the alphas, which is so ridiculous I'm not even going to address that.

Winston put his little nose in the sand. When he picked up his head, he gave me clumsy sandy kisses all over. He tried to nip me on the ear, but I was patient and didn't slap him even once. A puppy's life is hard enough without everyone losing patience.

Marcus gave Alison his number and Alison gave Marcus hers, writing with the pen whose top I had recently chewed. It was part of that incomprehensible ritual of people spewing numbers right and left instead of wearing proper ID tags on their collars.

As we traveled down the path a little farther, we came across a fenced-in area where smaller humans screamed and ran around. "It's a playground, monkey," said Alison. "See the swings and monkey bars? Yes, monkey bars! But not for you, monkey. You need opposable thumbs."

Did Alison think I lacked something? I would show her. I would get me some opposable thumbs, whatever those were, and I would demonstrate what a monkey girl could do with monkey bars.

As we got toward the bottom of the pathway, there were so many large patches of grass and a crosscurrent of different scents that I felt drunk with joy. I zigged and I zagged while Alison laughed. I peed, too, to make sure everyone knew I'd been here.

But wait, what was this? I sniffed around and felt an even bigger surge of joy. That unmistakable scent—Gus had been here, and just recently! The silky gray-and-black poodle-terrier mix, the one Cary Grant was lucky enough to look like. I pranced and danced.

Sure enough, around a bend of trees and shrubs, there he was, that handsome fella. He pulled on his leash to get near me, dragging along Tom and Greg and a baby in a carriage. His walk had a real movie-star swagger, although the way he pulled at his leash with his tongue hanging out the side of his mouth made him look a little comical for a moment.

"I was afraid you'd moved away," Alison called to Tom and Greg, a little huffy-puffy because I was tugging her so hard.

"We're back now," said Tom. "Things are easing up a bit here, and people are going back into the office."

The way Gus looked at me with his dark black eyes made my tail flutter. He was the most gentlemanly and classy doodle I had ever met. His silky hair was a glorious gray, and his dashing moustache was cleanly cropped.

Alison petted Gus, Tom petted me, and then all the humans cooed over the baby.

"Congratulations!" said Alison.

"The adoption came through during the pandemic, of all times. But it worked out perfectly."

"Can Dea see? She loves babies."

"Oh, he's cool with dogs," said Tom.

Alison picked me up and I wiggled and wiggled until I could get close enough to lick the baby's wrinkled little feet. His tiny mouth crinkled upward, and he made a happy gurgling sound. I've always been good with short humans, and this was certainly the shortest I'd ever seen.

"Can you believe our new park? It's glorious!" said Alison. "Hey, have you seen Jessie and Lola?"

"That's the pretty dog with the eyeliner? Haven't seen them in a while," said Tom. "But everyone seems to be coming back. They can't be far off."

What a day it was turning out to be. At the end of the lane was a short bridge crossing over the water, allowing us to continue deeper into the park. In the distance were more benches facing the river. There were so many benches, Alison would never get to knock wood on all of them in a zillion years.

From afar, I spotted Cody, the sweet pit bull, but she was lying next to her human, Ellen, on a long bench. We didn't want to disturb their apparent bliss. There were other dogs, too, that I had never seen before and was dying to get to sniff. Alison pulled me away, saying there'd be other days and other walks when I could meet them. "Otherwise, we'll be out here all night," she said, laughing.

The late afternoon had a beautiful orange glow, golden and calming. We walked back up toward the new promenade, taking the longest curving path—and it's a good thing we did, because around the bend came Ozzie the goldendoodle! Ozzie is a very jovial sort, and so is his human, Rosie. They met us halfway up the path. Alison bent down to hug Ozzie's belly, and she should have done that to Rosie, too, because those two have had lunch a few times and it would be a fine way to show that Alison was excited to see her. But you know humans; one can never count on them to do the right thing.

"Dea, you beautiful creature, you just missed your friend Iggy," said Rosie. I spun my head this way and that to catch a sight of Iggy the border collie, the breed that's supposed to be smarter than poodles, although I never trusted the methodology behind that assessment. Did you see what I did there? I used two very big words. If that's not smart, what is? And don't tell me about herding sheep again, because I can count them in my sleep.

"How's Delia doing?" asked Alison about Iggy's person.

"She's had a tough time with the lockdown," said Rosie. "She lost her job. She had to homeschool her kids. I think she was majorly depressed for a while, but she's coming out of it. She even dyed some of her hair purple."

"Is that a good sign or a bad sign? I mean, is it a cry for help?"

"No, it's a very nice shade of purple," said Rosie. "I think it shows she's getting her fun, adventurous spirit back. If it were a terrible green, I'd be worried, but I think she's okay."

"Oh, hey, I've been looking around for Jessie. Have you seen her? I know Dea wants to play with Lola."

Rosie looked uncomfortable. "I guess you haven't heard," she said. "She lost Lola a few weeks ago."

Alison clapped a hand to her mouth and started to leak a little. "I can't believe it," she said.

"Lola was fourteen. She had been sick. It was her time. I mean, it's never the right time, that's true, but . . . well, you know what I'm trying to say."

Alison had been so happy, and now she couldn't stop leaking. What was wrong? After Ozzie took Rosie for more of her walk, Alison scooped me up in her arms.

"I'm sorry, monkey, Lola's gone. She went over the Rainbow Bridge."

But . . . I wanted to see her again! I wanted to see her eyeliner eyes!

"I know, sweet girl, and I'm the worst person when it comes to losing someone you love, but you have to understand this is what happens. Death is a natural part of life. They don't really leave us, you know, because they mean so much to us that they live on, in here." She touched her chest, and I thought maybe it hurt again there, but she touched herself tenderly, not in pain.

Even Alba, mama? Is Alba still with us?

"Even Alba," said Alison, reading my mind in that scary way she has. "And David, and Grace, and my mother. We are lucky to have them in our lives, and then we have to let them go."

She leaked a whole bunch more, but my poodle hair is quite absorbent.

As we slowly made our way toward home, Alison turned back to look down the path at the playground for the shorter humans. She gazed longingly at the swings for big people.

"I wish we could, but it's too embarrassing," she said. "I'm too grown up for that."

I gave a little woof and pulled on the leash. It was a playground, Alison had told me, so let's play!

"Oh, I don't know, Dea . . ."

I kept pulling her down the path toward the planks for swinging.

"I haven't been on one of those since I was five or six," she said. "David used to push me. It was really an incredible feeling. But I don't know . . ."

She sat on a plank tentatively and drew me into her lap, where she held me tightly with one arm, facing me forward the way we do when we bench sit. We swayed back and forth on the swing, moving an inch or two each way, just enough to feel a gentle rocking motion.

Alison looked right and left to see if anyone was watching, and then she suddenly seemed not to care who saw us having fun. "Dea, shall we go higher?"

She grabbed onto the metal chain holding up the sides of the plank and swung us higher and higher, up toward the limitless sky. I hadn't felt that kind of strength from her in a while, even when she threw my favorite toy in the morning.

Higher and higher toward the sky without limit or fear. After all the isolation and all the empty store shelves, it felt liberating, like we were open to all new possibilities, leaving our doubts and fears behind in the wind. Alison laughed, and my mouth was slightly open like dogs do when they hang their heads out car windows to taste the wind, which Alison doesn't allow. It felt good to remember Lola and all the things we used to do together. Even though I couldn't sniff her anymore, I could see her very clearly, her eyes rimmed as if with flirty eye pencil, happily doing her pony dance for all the other dogs.

Alison squeezed me, just tightly enough.

"I love you completely, monkey girl," she whispered in my ear.

I knew what she meant.

Acknowledgments

I want to thank my brilliant editor, Jami Bernard, whose intellect, humor, patience, and teaching skills have taught me so much about writing, empowering me to write this book.

I want to thank my friend Judy Katz, who inspired me with the idea of writing this memoir entirely from my dog's point of view.

Thank you to Bill Adler for his encouragement along the way, and a special thank you to Tony Iatridis, the talented art director and web designer who made my beautiful new website and who has helped me in so many ways. Finally, thank you to all my friends who were cheering me on to write this book.

I am grateful to Lama Surya Das for writing such a beautiful and most inspiring book, *Awakening The Buddha Within: Tibetan Wisdom for the Western World* (Broadway Books, 1997). The wisdom in this book continues to keep me centered during the most difficult of times. It has proven to be invaluable in my life.

Of course, I would like to thank all of Dea's wonderful, remarkable dog friends, who motivated me to write about them in this memoir. But most importantly, I thank my incredible dog, Dea, for her endless love, humor, and "insights" about life. This book could not have been written without her by my side.

About the Author

ALISON RAND has a master of social work degree, but her eclectic professional background also includes copywriting, acting, voiceovers, and audiobook narration.

Alison's first book, *A Place Called Grace* (2018), traced her adventures while living in Italy as she struggled to find her footing as an actress. It is a humorous, hopeful, and bittersweet contemporary memoir that shows how a seemingly unmoored existence can find its solid center after all.

Alison is an exercise enthusiast, especially hiking and skiing. She is an avid dog person, and lives with her poodle, Dea, at home in Manhattan, where she was born and raised.

AlisonRandauthor.com
f facebook.com/AlisonRandAuthor